"I can think of no greater burden than to live without hope. But for many of us hope is nothing more than a fingers-crossed human act of wishful thinking. In this powerful book Becky encourages us to take a brutally honest look at all that is true about our lives—and in the midst of that unsettling picture she shows us the source of our real hope. For those who live with doubt and shadows, the gift of this book is solid, well-reasoned faith and the light of the Son of God himself."

SHEILA WALSH, author, Women of Faith keynote speaker

"I am very glad that Becky's book is being reissued. In my earliest days planting a church in Manhattan I discovered that her Christian vision had deep appeal to many of the most secular and skeptical people. I personally learned much from her for my own preaching and teaching. I highly recommend this volume."

TIMOTHY KELLER, senior pastor, Redeemer Presbyterian Church, New York City

"Few people have explored more profoundly than Rebecca Manley Pippert the uneasy gulf that separates modern secularism from traditional Christian interpretation of human nature. Ranging brilliantly from Camus to Freud and Nietzsche, Pippert diagnoses the various self-deceptions that people engage in to avoid the unpleasantness of true moral self-knowledge. The book is stunning. Not for a generation or more has anyone set forth so powerfully or movingly the Christian view that humanity's primary curse is a moral one and that the ultimate solution has already been made available to us."

DAVID AIKMAN, senior fellow, Ethics and Public Policy Center

"Rebecca Pippert speaks to the question that haunts me almost every day of my life: What difference does God make? Her answers are clear but not facile, honest but hopeful, and above all truly Christian. She helped me where I hurt, taught me where I am ignorant, and made me hopeful where I despair."

LEWIS B. SMEDES, author of *Forgive and Forget*

"Must reading for all who are searching for the meaning of life and are ready to do all that God's Spirit will reveal as necessary."

GEORGE A. MALONEY, author of *Called to Be Free*

"A challenging and hopeful book for those who are weary of playing God yet frightened of surrendering to grace."

MACRINA WIEDERKEHR, author of *A Tree Full of Angels*

"A no-nonsense, practical book for those who have failed and don't know what to do about it."

JAMIE BUCKINGHAM, author of *Run Baby Run*

"Carries the fundamental teachings and realities of Christ into the heart of our contemporary distress. . . . The teaching is deep, the stories realistic, instructive and uplifting. I finished with tears of gratitude to God for his indescribable gift."

DALLAS WILLARD, author of *Hearing God*

"Gritty realism, passionate love and humorous holiness fuse in these pages and energize mere reading into a lively conversation with [Pippert's] companions on the Way."

EUGENE H. PETERSON, author of *A Long Obedience in the Same Direction*

"This extraordinary book makes God's grace more amazing than ever, and you will find yourself 'lost in wonder, love and praise.' "

DAVID A. SEAMANDS, author of *Healing for Damaged Emotions*

REVISED EDITION

HOPE
HAS ITS
REASONS

The Search to Satisfy
Our Deepest Longings

REBECCA MANLEY PIPPERT
AUTHOR OF *OUT OF THE SALTSHAKER*

InterVarsity Press
Downers Grove, Illinois

InterVarsity Press
P.O. Box 1400, Downers Grove, IL 60515-1426
World Wide Web: www.ivpress.com
E-mail: mail@ivpress.com

InterVarsity Press® is the book-publishing division of InterVarsity Christian Fellowship/USA®, a student movement active on campus at hundreds of universities, colleges and schools of nursing in the United States of America, and a member movement of the International Fellowship of Evangelical Students. For information about local and regional activities, write Public Relations Dept., InterVarsity Christian Fellowship/USA, 6400 Schroeder Rd., P.O. Box 7895, Madison, WI 53707-7895.

Cover photograph: Chikara Amano/Photonica

ISBN 0-8308-2278-X

Printed in the United States of America ∞

Library of Congress Cataloging-in-Publication Data

Pippert, Rebecca Manley
  Hope has its reasons: the search to satisfy our deepest longings / Rebecca Manley
Pippert.—1st ed.
    p. cm.
  Includes bibliographical references.
  ISBN 0-8308-2278-X (paper : alk. paper)
    1. Christian life. I. Title.
BV4501.2 .P5546 2001
248.4—dc21
                                                                    2001024404

25 24 23 22 21 20 19 18 17 16 15 14 13 12 11 10 9 8 7 6 5 4 3 2 1
22 21 20 19 18 17 16 15 14 13 12 11 10 09 08 07 06 05 04 03 02 01

I dedicate this book with love and gratitude to my parents:

In memory of my father, who gave me the confidence and freedom to march to the beat of a Different Drummer.

To my mother, whose boundless love and dedication enabled me to trust in the Greatest Love of all.

Contents

Acknowledgments

It has been twelve years since I first published this book, and in that brief time the world has changed. Presidents and celebrities have come and gone. Ideas have been proposed and challenged. Wars have been won and lost. Fortunes have gone boom and bust. And so this book has also had to change.

But as I revised this book, it also became clear that much in it could stay the same for two important reasons: first, God doesn't change, and second, the central human problem has not changed. We may dress up the problem of what keeps us from God and call it by different names—disorder, dysfunction, addiction—but the traps and temptations have not changed much. There is a third thing that hasn't changed as well: God's ways of reaching out to us.

This book was written with two audiences in mind. I wrote it for thoughtful seekers who are willing to take an honest look at the problem of human nature and its possible ultimate solution. I also wrote it for Christians who are willing to take a deeper look at the various deceptions we engage in that keep us not only from true self-knowledge but from a deeper experience of God's grace.

I want to thank two people in particular who helped me in the original book: Os and Jenny Guinness, who worked tirelessly in providing loving support and editorial help. Their passionate concern for truth constantly challenged me to go back and rewrite where I was vague or off-center.

I also want to express my gratitude to and honor the late Professor Richard Wood. In all of my collegiate studies I can think of only one course that truly changed my life, and it was his. Indeed the seeds of this book began with his inspired lectures on Camus and Dostoyevsky my freshman year at Oklahoma State University. With his relentless honesty, his compassion for his students and his faith in God, he encouraged me always to ask the tough questions of life that eventually led to the production of this book.

Finally I thank my family: my wonderful husband, Dick, and my children, Elizabeth and David, who cheered and supported me all the way through.

There are two things in the book that I wish might have been different. First, many of the writers I drew upon did not have the sensitivity to gender that we have today. As I quoted them and used their ideas, there was no easy way to get around that lack. Second, I wish there had been time and space to develop the notion of evil on more than the individual level. But to develop the implications of systemic evil was beyond the scope of this book. The fact that it is not mentioned does not mean that it is not a critical issue for all of us.

1

The Problem with the World Is Me

The chief and only thing wrong with the world is man.
CARL GUSTAV JUNG

People have two things in common: We all want to be happy and we all want to be loved. And we cannot understand why something so simple should be so difficult. In fact, we may not even be able to articulate what we feel we desire and yet miss. To paraphrase Mark Twain, "You don't know quite what it is you do want, but it just fairly makes your heart ache you want it so."

Part of the ache comes from the fact that in spite of the glut of the mundane and the ugly, somehow we know we were made for something more. Something more seemed promised. There is more for us to live for, to embrace or to be embraced by. We are surely here to participate in something wider and deeper than we have yet realized. We want to know that our lives are significant, that it will make a difference that we have been here. So with the best of intentions we feverishly pursue happiness and significance, love and understanding. Is that too much to ask? Yet something blocks us from achieving such a reasonable goal.

A brilliant physicist once told me, "I thought establishing my career and becoming successful would be the toughest challenge of my life, so that was where I focused my energy. Now I see that was relatively easy compared to making my family life work and being able to communicate with my children. At work I write a memo and everything gets done. Yet I drive only thirty minutes to my home and all of the rules change. Why is it that I can relate easily to my colleagues and secretary, who aren't that important to me, yet I can't communicate easily to my children, who are everything to me? Why are the simplest things the hardest?"

Another friend, who is very competent professionally, feels very incompetent at romantic love: "I am my own worst enemy. At work I call the shots, I'm in charge and I am valued for my wise judgments. But in matters of the heart, I lose my footing. One moment I'm being dominated and constantly trying to please, and the next moment I am demanding and difficult. From nine to five I'm a grown-up. But at love I'm an adolescent. What blocks me from the maturity in love that I seek?"

Still another friend, who by our culture's standards has it all, recently asked me, "Why, in spite of all the success I have achieved both at work and at home, do I still feel a hollowness?"

Too often our very pursuit of happiness becomes our agony. It leaves us emptier and lonelier than ever. We know it's not the superficial, bubbly kind of happiness for which we long, the kind that would perhaps have satisfied us in our youth. We are wistful for something deeper that will satisfy our longing. But what is it that we want and how on earth are we to reach it? We sense that something is missing, even that something is wrong with us, but what it is we are not quite sure. And in times like our own, when the gap between ideals and conduct has grown so wide, that desire becomes all the more poignant.

Of course there has always been a gap between the ideals people espouse and the way they live, between knowledge and behavior, intellect and character. The difference today is not that the discrepancy exists but that our modern expectations do not cater to it. Ancients understood that it was only in admitting the gap between what you profess and how you perform that growth and maturity could take place. But not today. In a world where ideals of happiness are shaped by advertising and pop psychology, such an admission is thought too negative. We prefer our leaders and celebrities to have smiling faces, successful résumés, big bank accounts, perfect teeth—and never a hint of weakness, failure or self-doubt. We do not want to know that they too have to face the painful and the mundane.

So when our heroes fail, and the gap is glaring, we are shocked and feel betrayed. The error must have been in our faulty selection. We will be more careful next time when we raise someone to the status of hero. Yet we never seem to stop and ask what it is about human nature in the public eye that cannot seem to take the lights for too long without disappointing the audience. All we feel is a certain wordless sadness deepened by simplistic solutions that trivialize our problems and insult our intelligence.

In short, it is hard to live too long before we start asking, Is there something missing or wrong with our lives? Where do we go to find lasting happiness, and where is the power to help us reach it?

In this search most of us have had the experience of discovering new causes. They last awhile, bringing a certain zest and promise. But eventually we go on to the next thing. Somehow the small print of the reality never matches the billing in the headline. To deepen our confusion, people we respect adhere to quite different causes, yet each claims that his or her own is the answer. Forget the other ones, we are told. This one is it. And the louder and more confident their claims, the more followers they are able to pick up. Most of us finally conclude that our wisest approach is to look at life as honestly as we can and see if people's claims and causes fit the facts as we see them and have experienced them.

No one writes a book who does not have some truth to share or story to tell. I am no exception. The truth that has changed my life was coming to believe in God as shown in Jesus Christ. But I did not start from faith. On the contrary, I made my pilgrimage from unbelief to faith kicking and resisting all the way. And since my own journey began in skepticism, being encouraged to ask questions and never being asked to adopt belief blindly, I have chosen a similar approach in this book—for a particular reason.

Many believers and most unbelievers have a similar problem with regard to the Christian faith: They have never understood the realism of the Christian view of life and human nature. As a result, too many Christians end up with an inadequate faith. Many who are not Christians, on the other hand, end up with too little short-term happiness and too much long-term misery in their skepticism. This book is written for both.

What Difference Does It Make?
Over the years my faith has had to grow progressively more realistic, always confirming deeper levels of what the Bible had said all along. Like all new converts, I began with great excitement. I couldn't wait to tell the story, to see mountains move, lives change. I was ready. You're always ready at eighteen. Part of my zeal, no doubt, was a reflection of my age, perhaps also of temperament. But I had every confidence that God would do great things. And now, some thirty years later, I can say with certainty that he has.

What I didn't foresee were some of the rude surprises along the way. Most valuable of all have been challenges from thoughtful searchers and tough questions from critics looking at faith from the outside. For example, a conversation I once had with a Harvard professor summed up many of the questions and doubts that trouble people today.

"Even though I am an atheist," he said, "I genuinely admire people like you who take faith seriously. There is no question that the human race needs help. But honestly, Becky, isn't life the same whether we believe in God or not? Don't all of us long to be loved and understood? Don't we all try to make sense out of our lives and care about our health, our kids, our finances, whether we accept God or not?"

"Yes, that's true," I answered.

"Life is difficult for all of us," he went on. "I don't think cancer cells ask before entering a body, 'Excuse me. Are you a praying person?' And don't all of us, believers as well as skeptics, raise our children the best we can? And some make it, but when they don't, it leaves us with broken hearts and dashed hopes whether we believe in God or not."

"Of course!" I answered him.

"And don't believers fail morally? I grant that many of you do better in certain areas than we do. But I have met my share of religious people who were racists, gluttons, self-righteous and full of pride, all the while mouthing platitudes. And don't tell me they did not consider themselves real believers. Trust me, they did. Then what possible difference does God make?"

That certainly is the fundamental question. It is one we must ask ourselves with honesty, whether we believe or not. It's the one that has spurred me constantly in the exploration and journey of this book.

The professor was right. Life brings similar experiences to believer and unbeliever alike. He was right, too, that life is often difficult. It can be tough whether we believe in God or not. I was no stranger to suffering when I first became interested in faith. Yet curiously, although there is no such promise in the Bible, I think I half-expected that my relationship with God would cushion me from pain. But believers aren't exempt from pain. They experience illness, sexist bosses, unemployment, violence and marital problems just like everyone else.

The professor was unquestionably correct when he said that Christians fail morally too. I once heard an international businessman say, "I am on two boards. One is with a religious organization, and the other is with secular people. With the secular board members, I know that many are out for their own agenda. They manipulate and control and deceive. I know it, and so do they. But frankly, I've seen lots of the same controlling, manipulative, deceitful behavior on the religious board. The difference is not in the behavior but in the fact that the secular board members often acknowledge their motives, whereas the believers don't. The believers not only deny them but cover their motives with pious words. They talk spiritually, but they are playing the same game."

Making Ourselves the Exception
That sort of lesson in realism is one of the surprises I encountered in my journey of faith almost from the start. But the biggest surprise of all has been about myself. I have had to face up to what I am sure has been clear to everyone else all along: I am flawed. Mind you, I always knew theoretically that to be human was to be flawed—as in "hey, nobody's perfect." But as the years have gone by, I have had to face up to the specific and

undeniable evidence that I am my own worst case.

A psychiatrist has noted that all of us are engaged to one degree or another in a personal, ongoing battle with sin and vice, although we may not think of our conflicts with ourselves in those terms. This has been true for me. Take a somewhat trivial example. Recently I was terribly rushed and needed to get to the bank before closing. There were several cars ahead of me, and just as I drove up to the teller he informed me that the bank was now closed. I pleaded with him to make an allowance, just this once. He was polite but firm: the answer was no. Then I suggested it would be great customer service to extend the time by only a few minutes. He pointed to his watch, said he was sorry, but no. I left in a visible huff.

But as I considered my behavior I felt ashamed. Why should I be angry at him because I arrived late? How many times have I said to my children, "Just what is it about 'no' that you don't seem to understand?" Why should the closing rules apply to everyone else but me?

Granted, my anger didn't make me a murderer, any more than moments of envy or criticism of another have made me a criminal. But the seeds are there. And whether they were expressed as feelings, thoughts, speech or actions, the conclusion is inescapable: the struggle to master my flaws has not been quick or easy.

If these were the only incidents to report, they wouldn't be worth mentioning. Or if they took place eight weeks or eight months after I began walking seriously with God, then never mind. But these incidents took place many years after I came to know God. What these experiences and others have told me about myself is that left to my natural devices I will always be tempted to make an exception of myself. Again and again I have been brought face to face with the fact that no matter how profound my conversion, it has not yielded a finished product.

Perhaps most important, these painful lessons took me more by surprise than they should have. In fact, along with the reality of my flaws, I have been forced to face a startling lust for innocence. In theory, I have always agreed with C. S. Lewis that for anyone to insist on one's own innocence is about as reasonable as a "divorceé pretending to be a virgin." Nonetheless, that was exactly what I was guilty of.

What does all this mean? Am I just one more example of a religious person whose life does not match her words? Doubtless some devout soul would write me off as unspiritual. Doubtless some skeptics would acknowledge my sincerity but say it just goes to show that faith in God doesn't really change lives radically. Perhaps the sad fact is that although Christians think they have changed, they are just religious versions of the same people they have always been.

One thing we all agree on, whatever our perspective: no one likes hypocrisy. Faith, to have credibility, cannot mean adherence to beliefs that have no relation to behavior. There must be a vital connection between doctrine believed and life lived. That insistence is just as important for the unbeliever as for the believer. We all share the same humanity, which means that we share the same fundamental problems and need the same help and healing. We experience the same curiosity when a solution is offered. We have the same vested interest in seeing whether the solution works. We have all met new converts to various faiths who are passing through a honeymoon period in which life is filtered through a rose-tinted lens. Everything works as never before, they claim. Yet we know from experience that all but the most ardent zealot will be tempered by the harsh realities of life.

So once again we come back to the question, what real difference does faith make? But this time there is an added sting in the tail. Is the truth simply that just as human problems are the same, so are the answers? Could it be a case of calling the problem and the answer by different names? Thus one person's sin is another person's neurosis, one man's priest is another's shrink, one woman's need for confession is another's need for therapy.

The fact is that the languages of faith and psychology do overlap in startling ways. And since most of us are bilingual these days, we are tempted to ask why we don't just admit it. Our problems and answers are the same, only the labels change to suit our traditions and preferences. So if some people want to say that God is their "thing," then fine. Let them. But they should realize, the suggestion runs, that *God* is only another word for the human need for love and understanding. "God," for them, is the equivalent of the therapy or political cause that gives meaning and purpose to their lives.

Piety or Pain?

The skeptic and the believer are therefore not as far apart over such questions as many people think. They are plagued by the same problems and need the same answers. Believers and unbelievers alike end up asking the same question as the professor: what difference does God really make?

A friend put it succinctly. "Why can't I get my inside to match my outside? I started my walk with God full of enthusiasm. But I'm slowly realizing I may not love God as deeply or as consistently as I once thought. I understand the price involved in embracing faith fully, far better than I did when I first believed. Yet I sometimes feel less inclined to pay the price. I sense a gap between the promise of God in Scripture and the reality of my own performance."

It is ironic that today many Christians find such candor shocking, when for the early Christians it was elementary in their expectations. Too many contemporary Christians have reversed this realism. They present themselves as finished products; all new and nothing old, all success and no failure.

I have one friend who comes across as so spiritual he never seems to have a bad day. He sprinkles every sentence with pious words, whether they fit the occasion or not. Just seeing him gives me a spiritual inferiority complex and a headache. One time he came striding in triumphantly and said, "Hello, Becky. Praise God! How are you? The Lord is good! My car was totaled. Thank you, Jesus!"

"Yes, yes," I said rather routinely, "everything is fine . . . What did you just say?"

"God is good," he replied.

"I got that part. But what about your car?"

"It was totaled last night. Praise the Lord!" he answered with a glow.

I was shocked. "But that's terrible!" I exclaimed.

"Not when you know the Lord!" he retorted. And off he went on an apparent celestial cloud.

He left me to ponder some rather earthly questions. Is that the kind of behavior we are to emulate if we trust in God? Does faith mean we can't acknowledge fear, doubt, anger or frustration? Does loving God mean that we so live in the world of the Spirit that we are oblivious to daily problems and rise above the less spiritual types who struggle with such mundane things as totaled cars? Does being a believer mean that the ambiguity of life disappears magically and that to acknowledge concerns and worries reflects our spiritual weakness? Does adopting a spiritual stance mean a pain-free, tensionless existence?

In my agnostic days, that type of pious behavior made me want to run for the hills. In fact, when I came close to faith, I wavered before making a commitment because I was afraid such "holy" behavior would be required of me. If this were the case, I knew I was in big trouble because no matter how devout I'd become there was no way I could pull it off. What's more, the thought that I would be spending eternity hanging around people like that didn't thrill me.

Where Have All the Prophets Gone?
The Harvard professor's question is intensified even further if we add to the picture a reminder of the times in which we live. By anyone's standards, it is safe to say that we are living in extraordinary, even crazy, times.

In the not so distant past the church all too often seemed to be singing the secular song, and the prophets who came closest to biblical sermons were from the so-called secular world. For example, *Time* magazine did a cover story in 1987 entitled "Whatever Happened to Ethics? Assaulted by Sleaze, Scandal and Hypocrisy, America Searches for Its Moral Bearings."[1] Where did they see signs of the crisis? *Time* pointed out that America was no longer in the introspective "me" decade of the 1970s but in the materialistic "my" decade of the 1980s.

In a commencement address at Colby College in 1981, Garry Trudeau, the creator of the comic strip *Doonesbury,* quoted the historian Christopher Lasch as saying we live in a society "where men wish to be not so much esteemed as envied."[2] CBS anchorman Dan Rather did a radio spot in the 1980s on "Whatever Happened to Sin?" Ellen Goodman, a syndicated columnist, wrote a column entitled "The Goodness of Guilt." The late Meg Greenfield, who wrote essays for *Newsweek,* did a piece on "The Possibilities of Moral Absolutes." Most powerful of all was Ted Koppel's commencement address at Duke University, in which he said:

> We have actually convinced ourselves that slogans will save us. Shoot up if
> you must, but use a clean needle. Enjoy sex whenever and with whomever
> you wish, but wear a condom. No! The answer is no! Not because it isn't cool
> or smart or because you might end up in jail or dying in an AIDS ward. But
> no because it's wrong, because we have spent five thousand years as a race of
> rational human beings, trying to drag ourselves out of the primeval slime by
> searching for truth and moral absolutes. In its purest form, truth is not a
> polite tap on the shoulder. It is a howling reproach. What Moses brought
> down from Mount Sinai were not the ten suggestions.[3]

But times have changed. Such secular prophets are being rejected because their moral reasoning sounds preachy to our postmodern ears. "Thou shalt not be intolerant" is the new commandment, the new battle cry. We have gone beyond the common understanding of pluralism—the belief that no single explanation or view of reality can account for all the phenomena of life. Modern Americans now believe that not only must we be sympathetic to a differing point of view from ours, but we must accept it as equally as valid as our own.

Film director Jane Campion, who frequently focuses on women's issues, has created *Holy Smoke*, a film with a quintessentially postmodern message. The story focuses on a concerned mother whose daughter has become involved in an Eastern cult while on holiday in India. Because of her increasingly bizarre behavior, the desperate mother finally asks a "deprogrammer" to help her daughter come to her senses. The tables are surprisingly turned around, however, when in spite of his successful track record the young woman strips the deprogrammer of his power psychologically, spiritually and emotionally. Ultimately, this caring but overly confident macho man is reduced almost to a thumb-sucking little boy. Why is the attack against him so savage?

Some may find the film objectionable because of its overt sexuality and strong language. But there are much more serious issues at stake here. Among the many layers of meaning to Campion's film, the strongest message is this: to deprogram anyone from *any* belief is the one unforgivable sin in today's culture. Why? Because in contemporary culture *nothing is worse* than supposing that another's belief is flawed or inferior. It's perfectly fine to have one's own beliefs. But to make a judgment that presupposes that all beliefs aren't equal is intolerable. Tolerance (which today is defined as the assumption that all beliefs are equally valid) is sacrosanct.

Is the Church Different from the Culture?

Americans, we are told, are the most religious people in the developed world. More than 90 percent tell pollsters that they believe in God, 43 percent say they attend religious services once a week, and 58 percent report that religion is very important to them.[4] But what does this really mean? When so many say they are motivated by religious values, do those values have any identifiable content? When society at large enshrines "tolerance" and reluctance to make moral judgments as the highest virtues, what do those who attend weekly services at churches and synagogues hear?

James Davison Hunter answers that question in the spring 2000 edition of *The Public Interest*, suggesting that the secular worldview is influencing believers far more than the reverse.[5] Hunter examines the moral education curricula at U.S. churches (evangelical, mainstream and Catholic) and synagogues and finds that the old categories of sin, repentance and redemption are out and the therapeutic language of self-esteem and self-love are in. Building self-esteem has become a substitute for serious moral reasoning and self-examination. The nationally syndicated writer Mona Charen, reflecting on Hunter's findings, writes: "The triumph of the therapeutic has left millions of Americans without the mental equipment to make moral choices. And when sin does rear its ugly head, our national response, both secular and religious, is to call in the shrinks."

The Problem with the Universe Is Me

Does God make a difference? Despite all I have said, despite all the hypocrisies and the inconsistencies we have examined here, the Bible still has the nerve to proclaim yes, and again yes! But there is one unavoidable condition for experiencing change. We have to face up to the truth, and above all to the fact that the problem is us.

The paradox of the human condition is that it contains both the good and the bad, the generous and the self-centered, the honest and devious. This paradox makes the detection of our flaws particularly difficult—but particularly important. We can look around us and see how much genuine kindness there is. Most parents are overwhelmed by the depth of love they feel for their children, their spontaneous ability to give unselfishly. In every community one finds quiet heroism and self-sacrifice. Most of us try hard to have warm relationships at home, to be productive, responsible citizens and workers. We mostly admit that we have our nasty bits, to be sure. But on the whole, we're in pretty good shape, aren't we?

The answer, to an extent, is yes, because what we see is true. There is something truly wonderful and remarkable about us all. We have a capacity for love, an appreciation of beauty and moments of genuine courage. But unfortunately, that's not the whole story. We want to believe that the essential "us" is who we are in our best moments, when everything is going our way, when nothing is thwarting or threatening us. We want to believe that we are what we project to the world: nice, respectable, competent people who have it all together. Fortunately or unfortunately, life doesn't let us get away with our charade. Sooner or later, whether through a difficult relationship with a berating boss, a demanding spouse or a difficult child, or simply through overwhelming or infuriating circumstances, we are confronted with our darker side.

Has it ever struck you as odd that for all our sophistication today, we have a remarkably naive understanding of human nature? Having lived through the end of history's most murderous century, we flatter ourselves that we are basically good people who occasionally do bad deeds. The founders of the United States were not so naive. The very political institutions they constructed for us, founded on concepts like "checks and balances," are testimony to their assumption that human nature has a root of evil that unchecked can grow to terrifying proportions. People with power cannot be trusted too far. History hardly indicates that our problem has changed—rather, it shows that we have developed short memories. We are struggling with the symptoms of an age-old disease that we have lost the capacity to diagnose.

Once G. K. Chesterton was asked to contribute to a series in the London *Times* on the question "What is the problem in the universe?" He answered, "I am. Sincerely, G. K. Chesterton." Such realism is often found in those who have experienced tragedy. This came home to me in a conversation with a friend who is a recovering alcoholic. He told me of the first time he went to a meeting of Alcoholics Anonymous.

"I walked into the room," he said, "and the first thing I sensed was there wasn't a single person in the room who had not suffered. They had come face to face with their weakness, their inability to change without outside help. They had failed, and yet there was this sense of tremendous hope. They really believed that God could help me, and they wanted to stand by me as I sought to stop drinking. They embraced me as I was, a drunk, but they were certain that I could be changed. I felt like I was in a fellowship of the wounded, but the wounded and healed."

I was so moved by his description that I burst out, "But Bob, that is the best description of church that I've ever heard!"

He smiled and continued, "Let me tell you about the times I went to church during my drinking days. The message was always very polite but firm: 'Come back when you have your act together.'"

"Then why isn't the church like an AA meeting?" I asked.

He answered, "Because we don't really believe that the problem rests in us. We think that the problem is 'out there'; we are good and respectable in here. We do not admit that the rot is in us too."

Are you willing to grant that, whether believers or not, many of us have not really faced up to the human predicament, let alone our own? Perhaps that describes you, as it certainly did me. No book is for everyone. This one is written for people who are frustrated and left with longings because of the gaps in their lives, who want encouragement and hope as they live their lives in the lab between promise and performance. This book is written for those who want to examine the things that block us from finding the love and happiness we seek. And it is written for those who are willing to ask whether these wistful longings of the heart are actually within our reach or serve only to mock us. Is life merely one long, absurd pursuit of things we can never have, or does hope have its reasons? That is what we must find out. So if you share my refusal to live an unexamined life, I invite you to join me in exploring some of the lessons from my personal journey.

2

The Lie That
We're OK

If a way to be better there be,
it lies in taking a full look at the worst.
THOMAS HARDY

Many of us live most of our lives without ever getting below the surface. But sooner or later we usually weary of sleepwalking. Something finally jolts us out of our reverie. and we begin to ask ultimate questions about the meaning of our lives. We know that we desire happiness, purpose and love. Yet the simplest desires seem to be beyond our reach. Is there anyone who has identified what blocks us from what we seek but cannot find?

Albert Camus has done so through Clamence, the central character in his novel *The Fall*.[1] Clamence starts out superficially content, but eventually he senses that something in his life is lacking, something about it is not right. As we follow the logic of his disquiet, we see a progression in his inner pilgrimage. And that progression can help us as we try to explore the even deeper questions of the human predicament.

I first read *The Fall* in a philosophy of literature course my freshman year of college. Although I had a newfound faith in Christ, it would not be an exaggeration to say that this book changed my life. Camus's ruthless, scathing analysis of human nature forced me to take a deeper, more honest look at my own humanity than I ever had previously. I believe Camus has examined human nature as deeply as any modern prophet.

Clamence is a respected Paris lawyer, a pleader of noble causes and utterly secure in his self-esteem. He never accepted bribes, entered into shady deals or attempted self-promotion through publicity. He tried his best to be decent and generous and to give everyone a fair shake. "You would really have thought that justice slept with me every night," he remarked. Privately, he was a sexual libertine; but since his intention was never to hurt anyone, and because he reasoned "Boys will be boys," he certainly did not feel himself to be a candidate for judgment. In short, he was a modern person.

All of this changes one day when he hears a young suicide plunge into the Seine River and does nothing to rescue her. At this moment he is given a searching look into who he really is. His indifference and laziness during the crisis became, he says later, the "bitter waters of my baptism." He began to observe himself, and he did not like what he saw. The unmasking started at the level of simple behavior: his irritation when someone interrupted one of his stories, his intolerance of fools or anyone who disagreed with him, his inability to be faithful to any woman no matter how devoted. The more he observed, the more he wished he had not. But it was too late. For all his brilliant discourses on justice and moral reasoning, he finally says, "It hurts to confess it, but I'd have given ten conversations with Einstein for an initial rendezvous with a pretty chorus girl. It's true, of course, that after the tenth rendezvous, I was longing for Einstein or a serious book."

What Clamence slowly came to see was the fundamental deceitfulness of human nature. "I was not simple," he confesses, for "modesty helped me to shine, humility to conquer, and virtue to oppress." He describes the sign he would put over his house to describe himself: "a double face, a charming Janus, and above it, the motto of the house, 'Don't rely on it.'"

Perhaps if I paused at this point and asked some Christians how they would diagnose Clamence's problem, they would respond, "Well, it's perfectly clear. The rogue is a sinner and he's struggling with guilt." Someone would murmur "Amen!" and that would be that.

And if I were to ask nonbelievers for their opinion, they might respond, "Look, the guy's become a bit neurotic because he didn't try to save the woman. He probably had some unresolved hostility toward his mother that he needs to work through."

But is either side any wiser for the analysis? What if I were to press a little further: But what does it really mean to say someone is a sinner or neurotic? We all have our dialect, be it psychobabble or "the language of Zion"—but how often do we stop to ask what many of our terms really mean?

We need to take a deeper look.

The Hiding Animal

One of Camus's central insights about human nature is that all humans live in hiding from themselves. We think, speak and act in "bad faith" because we do not want to face the truth. We are terrified of being discovered by others—and perhaps above all of unmasking ourselves—because we cannot face the judgment that we are responsible for our inner condition. Consequently we live a life of denial.

What Camus describes as "bad faith" and modern psychology as "denial" has been given much attention in modern thought. Allowing that psychology holds a sometimes absurdly elevated position in modern society, what it has to say about human nature and denial is deeply instructive for our exploration.

Denial is a garden-variety term used for a type of psychological defense mechanism, or strategy, that people use to shield themselves from painful truths they would rather not face. Denial is hard to pin down exactly because its deepest dynamics are hidden. It is also very complex. But most psychologists agree that in reaction to the deepest pain and conflict, a common human response is to deny the truth of our experience and feelings.[2] Most of us, as the nineteenth-century Danish Christian philosopher Søren Kierkegaard says in *The Sickness unto Death,* would rather tranquilize ourselves with the trivial.

In other words, neither modern psychology at its best nor modern writers like Camus support the superficial notion that all is well with us human beings. Far from it; we only begin to view ourselves accurately if we confront our deceitfulness. We all have painful, hidden, unacceptable feelings that we do not want to acknowledge (jealousy, hatred, anger, competitiveness, inadequacy). We all try hard to avoid these inadmissible impulses because they threaten our preferred image of ourselves or our loved ones.

You might say, then, that denial is one of the mental tricks we unconsciously use to save us from feeling what we are really feeling. The obvious case is the alcoholic who says, "I'm just a heavy drinker." Or the parents of a troubled child who have a terrible struggle facing reality, partly because it means facing painful feelings about the child and partly because it entails equally painful feelings about their own parenting. It is very difficult, of course, to be around people who use the strategy of denial, because what is so clear to everyone else is the last thing they will acknowledge. Sometimes we feel they are insulting our intelligence by denying what is so clear. But the strategy of denial means they have hidden their own feelings from themselves. The feelings are literally inaccessible.

The lesson to be underscored again and again is that to paper over a hidden feeling is not to get rid of it. Hidden impulses may be denied, but that does not make them go away. In fact, the more we deny them, the more they pop up later in disguised forms. The end product of our denial is behavior that contains our unacknowledged feelings, but in concealed forms: depression, irrational anger, anxiety, obsessional attachments and so on. Or the symptoms could be physical. What we forget is that our symptoms are masks of the feelings we are trying to avoid. So our denial compounds the problem. We carry not only the weight of our unacknowledged feelings but the extra baggage of the symptoms they trigger.

A Defense for All Seasons

The most commonplace type of denial is the kind we practice in relation to our parents and brothers and sisters. I know a woman who feels emotionally abandoned by her father. He is famous and highly respected nationally, but he's never been there for her. She can't remember a single key event in her life to which he came. But she couldn't handle the intolerable disillusionment of realizing that the person she wanted to believe in was flawed; that she was so intensely angry with someone she loved so much.

As we saw, however, to deny anger is not to eliminate it. Denial just forces the anger to erupt in other forms. One defense mechanism this woman used in her attempt to bury her anger was to idealize her father to almost mythic proportions. It was as if she were telling herself, *How can I be angry with one so perfect?*

Another symptom of my friend's denial led in the direction of what psychologists call "displacement"—the shifting of our feelings from someone who is the real source of the pain to someone else. She frequently remarked, "I don't know why, but every man I date I instantly pick apart. I'm so critical of men." It took her a long time to realize it was not the men she was angry with, it was her father. But it was unacceptable to her to be angry at her father, so she transferred her hostility to a "safe" target: her date.

It is always hard to see our parents as they really are. We feel disloyal and guilty just acknowledging that they are human beings with limitations, like ourselves. My friend's denial was reinforced by her need to preserve a secure image of her father and thus to keep her own world safe as well. But denial does not work. It only causes our symptoms to become more destructive.

Problems Without Answers and Answers Without Problems
Several years ago I had the opportunity to audit several graduate-level courses in psychology at Harvard. Overall I was struck by two things. First, the students were extraordinarily open and candid about their problems. It wasn't uncommon to hear them say, "I'm angry," "I'm afraid," "I'm jealous." The notion that "transparency" in relationships solves everything can be a dangerous illusion, but their admission of problems was certainly the opposite of what I have been saying about denial. Second, their openness about their problems was matched only by their uncertainty about where to find the resources to overcome them. Having confessed, for example,

their inability to forgive someone who had hurt them, how could they then resolve the problem by forgiving and being kind and generous instead of petty and vindictive?

One day after class, I dropped in on a Bible study group in Cambridge. It would be unfair to overdraw the contrast, but it was striking. No one spoke openly about his or her problems. There was a lot of talk about God's answers and promises, but very little about the participants and the problems they faced. The closest thing to an admission was a reference to someone who was "struggling and needs prayer."

To overstate it, the first group seemed to have all the problems and no answers; the second group had all the answers and no problems.

But what does it sound like to others when you have all the answers and no problems? It sounds like "happy talk"—cheery, blithe and not quite believable. I felt as if I were in a room of radiant "finished products." The atmosphere lacked reality, probably because strong elements of denial were present. Perhaps more than they realized, the Bible study members were "suppressing" the truth.

This kind of suppression of unpleasantness is common in certain religious circles in America, where the expectation is that we must smile, be upbeat and always be victorious. One reason for this is that amid the stress of our complex society we are insecure and afraid. Afraid that if we share who we are or what we are really feeling, we might lose our standing in the eyes of others, or God, or ourselves. If we expose our weakness, everyone will see we are not as mature in faith as was thought. So we disguise our deepest fears and problems even from ourselves.

Denial in the Devout

Is there anything special about denial in the lives of Christian believers? I think there is. Denial in the lives of religious believers can be the most complex denial of all. Why? Because as the Bible and leading atheists such as Marx, Nietzsche and Freud agree, religion itself can be the ultimate form of denial. Religion for Marx was an "opiate" and for Freud an "illusion." But these are only echoes of Pascal's term *diversion,* and all their criticisms pale beside the Bible's. The heart, said the prophet Jeremiah, is "deceitful above all things" (Jeremiah 17:9).

That is certainly the taproot of the problem, although there are various reasons that religious believers are susceptible to denial. One is that we aren't sure what happens to our humanity once we believe in God. We say to ourselves, *I couldn't possibly be struggling with that problem. I'm a believer now.* And the fact that we are still struggling can be confusing. On the one hand, we claim that God has changed us; on the other, we see we still have problems. We mistakenly think that to admit faults means that nothing has happened after all.

Another reason we resort to denial has to do with the misguided notion that to be religious means that we are always nice, or at least we must always appear to be nice. In this case we have a double blindness—one we've inherited from the human race and one we've picked up from the American heresy of "niceness." I am not talking here about goodness or integrity, being loving or practicing simple courtesy. I am talking about the importance we attach to being "nice"—the idea that to be a believer means we hardly admit to having a bad day, we never admit that we get furious, we just smile if our car gets totaled because we must be nice. Niceness distances us from the truth and our fellow human beings.

That doesn't mean we have license to act out everything we're feeling. Nor does it hinder us from striving toward becoming loving, kind, gentle, godly people. But to become the things we strive for, we must be honest and admit where we fall short.

In this regard the denial used by those who are not believers may actually be easier to deal with than denial by those who are. The former don't have as much invested in their "respectability" as the latter, who cover their problems, pretending they are not there.

The more I explore the subtlety of denial, the more I realize that we are all afraid of facing ourselves as we really are. To embrace the whole of us, our dark side as well as the light, is just too painful. We try to "think positively" so that we can leap ahead into the solution as a means of escaping from the problem. In Carl Jung's brilliant image, the person who tries to get away from his inferiority in this way wants to "jump over his own shadow"—his own hidden negative qualities, which Jungian psychology calls the "shadow." There is truth in the old cliché after all. We really are afraid of our own shadows.

What is so puzzling is that Christians can make profound statements about "sin" in theory and still distance themselves from its reality in practice.

For example, I know a woman who is a very angry, difficult person. Once she really let me have it, in a nonstop, high-decibel diatribe. I listened carefully, and where I could honestly acknowledge what I thought was my fault, I did. Later I told her that although I loved her, I was deeply troubled by her style and some of the harsh content of her attack. When I recounted to a friend what I'd said to her, he surprised me by saying, "Yes, Becky, I know you want to love her."

That was all it took to break through my denial. I saw in a flash that though I wanted to love her, the truth was I didn't even like her. In fact, I couldn't stand her. There are other difficult people in my life I do love, but not this one. Why did I say just the opposite? Was I being intentionally dishonest? No, I didn't recognize my true feelings even though they were right under the surface. I was denying them because to acknowledge to myself such an intense dislike for someone threatened my view of myself as the loving person I longed to be.

But to be honest about the way I really felt brought a great sense of relief. Jesus wasn't kidding when he said the truth shall set you free. It wasn't that I abandoned my determination to love her, or that I went to her in my new freedom and said in a blaze of glory, "I finally figured it out: I can't stand you! You make me sick!" It was that now I knew where I needed God's help. How could I ask for help for a problem I hadn't acknowledged?

Among the more curious forms of denial is taking a specific problem and exaggerating it into an unrealistic condition. We say, "I'm a mess," or "I'm hopeless," which sounds like a candid confession but actually blurs the problem and becomes a way to sidestep responsibility. One terribly clever form of denial is, when criticized, to dodge the issue by throwing the onus back on the critic—saying, for example, "Ah, yes, I hear your obvious anger" (which lets us off the hook).

It is very important to break the cycle of denial, because the first step to victory comes only when we say, "Yes, I'm sorry to admit it, but that anger [competitiveness, jealousy, lust] is mine." In other words, only when we own up to a problem can we hope to overcome it. If we insist we have no problem, the problem remains both ours and unconquered. Merely to say "Nobody's perfect" just doesn't cut it. Only when we are specific and make ourselves directly responsible do we break the iron chain of denial and take that first step toward victory.

Most of us try to overcome scars or problems of the past by putting them out of our mind. At first sight, owning up to painful truth looks like the worst thing that could happen to us. In reality, however, it's the best, because we have no hope of ever finding a solution if we will not admit we have a problem. There is just no way to jump over that step. There is no shortcut. We humans are remarkable in the energy, deftness and sheer brilliance we show in trying to avoid that one clear step: honest admission of our flaws. We prefer the easier—but far more insidious—path of denial.

The Cost of Innocence

Camus's second insight into human nature is that we not only live in denial, we go further to claim a pretended innocence. "The idea that comes most naturally to man, as if from his very nature, is the idea of his innocence. . . . We are all exceptional cases. We all want to appeal against something. Each of us insists on being innocent at all costs, even if he has to accuse the whole human race and heaven itself." The problem is, according to Camus, "we can't assert the innocence of anyone, whereas we can state with certainty the guilt of us all."

Camus is right on target. Feigned innocence is a form of denial several layers deeper. We are not merely refusing to acknowledge our problems. We are going one step further and asserting our complete innocence. In order to justify ourselves we go to any length and pull out all the stops to appear blameless. Which makes it inevitable that we project our problems onto others, making them the culprits because we cannot bear to face the problem in ourselves.

The strategy of feigned innocence begins with the paradox of so-called innocent guilt. "Gee," we say, "I don't have problems." But when pushed, we give a contorted response: "I didn't do it, and it's your fault anyway." Thus our desire to prove our own innocence usually leads to harsh and critical judgment of others because we project our guilt and our problems outward. Feigned innocence grows into a classic way of dealing with guilt: scapegoating.

One of the most sobering examples of feigned innocence can be found in Robert J. Lifton's The Nazi Doctors.[3] Lifton points out that the worst horrors of Nazism were not perpetrated by the culturally deprived and uneducated but by physicians, lawyers and the professional elite. The great philosopher Martin Heidegger, for example, signed up with the Nazis. Ezra Pound, a brilliant and sensitive poet, was eventually consumed with hatred and racism and became a propagandist for Hitler and Mussolini.

Most chilling is Lifton's portrayal of the routineness of the lives of the doctors he interviewed. Hannah Arendt has aptly spoken of "the banality of evil." The doctors were participants in one of the vilest outbreaks of evil this planet has ever witnessed. How could they do it? How could those trained in the name of healing torture and kill? How could they justify the kind of behavior where "ordinary people can commit demonic acts"? That is what Lifton sought to find out.

While the doctors occasionally betrayed pockets of guilt, he reports, they generally tried "to present themselves to me as decent people who tried to make the best of a bad situation. And they wanted a confirmation from me in this view of themselves." They couldn't bear to face their guilt, so they denied it, feigned innocence and projected their guilt by blaming it on the system: "the chaotic, complex conditions of Auschwitz."

Such feigned innocence led to a depth of moral blindness that is staggering. Lifton writes, "Yet none of them—not a single former Nazi doctor I spoke to—arrived at a clear, ethical evaluation of what he had done, and what he had been a part of." This denial of responsibility, along with their projection of guilt onto the system around them, was part and parcel of the evil in which they participated. It was the means by which they were able to enter into it in the first place.

But it is not only in extreme cases that the drive for innocence is so strong. Mundane, everyday examples are all around us, especially in today's climate. The late Meg Greenfield, then a columnist for Newsweek magazine, wrote an article some years ago that is as relevant today as it was then. She mused that 1987 was a year when the "parade of semi-penitents" and the "no-fault confession" truly became an art form.[4] First, there was a presidential confession majestically delivered after a major faux pas: the president stepped forward, grim-faced, with cameras rolling, and said, "I accept full responsibility." He made it sound so courageous, she wrote, as if his words were the ultimate act of statesmanship and valor. But wait a minute. What was happening? The focus was suddenly shifting to how courageous it was for him to take responsibility. So is responsibility dodging an option for the president too—or at least for his media handlers? Clever. Even our admission of guilt can be orchestrated as a way of making us seem guiltless.

Greenfield also examined other public confessions of televangelists and politicians. In all the cases, whether religious or secular, she noted, the hidden message was that these people were so busy doing important, good things that they should not be held accountable for their wrong behavior. Of course they were sorry for any pain they might have inadvertently caused. What's more, they looked so sad that we started to wonder if we were making unreasonable demands on these good, giving, busy people. We felt embarrassed to ask, "Just one more question . . . and we don't want to belabor this and we understand it was at a time when you were deeply involved with the emergency famine relief program and you had a broken leg and the rectory has just burned down, but if you don't mind going over that part about the $800,000 just one more time?" Repeatedly, Greenfield wrote, prominent wrongdoers had used the "rigged system" dodge to deflect responsibility. ("I was the victim of a hostile takeover," "I was the victim of the press," or "The Devil made me do it.")

What is striking is how little has changed. All that is sadly required to make Greenfield's article relevant is to insert new names from this year's headlines.

The Rise of the Alibi Industry
Have you noticed how the word *innocent* has become all the rage recently? A senator, commenting on the sexual misbehavior of some military personnel, remarked, "They're just boys looking for innocent fun."

Most of us have the same offhand effrontery to believe in our own inno-cence, and contemporary culture has raised the "alibi industry" to new heights of productivity. We operate, albeit nervously at times, out of an assumption of our own innate goodness. Yes, we may admit foibles here and there—such admissions only underscore how conscientious we are—but on the whole we think we are pretty good chaps. The irony, of course, is that we rarely feel the same way about anyone else. For example, News-week did a survey on whether Americans believe in the afterlife. Seventy-six percent believed that they were going to heaven, but far fewer believed that others would be there to join them.[5] It seems to be the American way to assume that if there is a heaven, we will surely be there. But frankly, we can't be sure about anyone else. We know them too well.

What makes us think we're different? Why is it that we are able to see the splinter in someone else's eye but not the beam in our own?

Innocence in the Devout

The distinctive form of denial in believers is paralleled by a distinctive form of feigned innocence. In fact, there are reasons some believers have more trouble in this area than most people around them. For one thing, believers often confuse being godly with being innocent. But to be devoted to God does not mean we are suddenly blameless and exempt from ulterior motives. To pretend innocence in order to prove we are spiritual is not only to live in unreality but to make worse an already bad situation. Besides pride, the desire to appear innocent is one of the most dangerous religious impulses of all. Not only do we conceal our problem with excuses and project it onto others; worse still, we make sure that our defects can never receive the treatment they require.

A friend of mine told me of the rise and fall of the pastor of a thriving church. He was a gifted preacher, but he was also an autocrat who made decisions without consulting with other people. If people wanted to discuss a decision he'd made, he became angry and hurt and made them feel as if they were disloyal and challenging his authority.

Yet all the time he was fragile underneath. So he needed praise and pos-itive feedback. He was frequently exhausted from overcommitment and from pushing himself so hard, but he wouldn't delegate. He perceived himself as unable to say no to anyone because he cared so much about people. But the truth was that he had to be in charge. In the end he became resentful toward those who had invited him to minister, without ever realizing that he was the one ultimately responsible for his decisions.

These patterns became the seeds of his downfall. The final events began when the church voted against his proposal to build a huge new sanctuary at once, voting instead to build as the money came in. (The wonderful part is that the money did come in and the sanctuary is now built.) But the pastor couldn't rejoice. He was angry that the vestry had not endorsed the proposal exactly as he framed it. He told the church staff the next week that he felt humiliated and unsupported and was considering whether he should resign because they had challenged his authority. They tried to explain that consulting together on a decision was no affront to him. And they tried to suggest carefully that to be a leader doesn't mean being right every time.

But their advice fell on deaf ears, and it was about that time that he started making offhand comments about getting old, his hair thinning and so on. Before long a woman from the congregation, with enormous needs of her own, came into his office and told him she had backed his proposal even if the church hadn't. And by the way, she had always found him terribly attractive. So an affair began; it was discovered, and he resigned.

What went wrong? What brought the minister down was not his sexual infidelity. The problem started earlier, with his failure to face up to the truth in himself. He was angry that the church wouldn't agree with his plan. But his anger was unacknowledged, his pride unconfessed, his insecurities unfaced. And then what could be more human than his doubts about his physical appeal? He realized that he was losing his power as he saw himself getting older.

Welcome to the human race! The pastor could have acknowledged that fact and learned to live as a good sport with what we all must face. Instead he denied the march of time and frantically sought to affirm that he was just as youthful and attractive as ever. Thus in seeking to assuage his needs through the strategy of denial, he flouted reality and destroyed himself and those he loved.

Tragically for him as a pastor ("shepherd"), he spiritualized his denial by blaming his congregation and accusing them of disobedience to God. "How terrible," he said, "when God's people disobey God by challenging their pastor." He was taking something dark and making it darker, while putting himself in a seemingly spiritual light. When the time came for him to make a public statement to the church, he began with a "confession" that slowly became transformed into a subtle condemnation of the church: The real problem was the burden of ministry—not getting long enough vacations; a system that demanded too much from its leaders. He said it so cleverly that few noticed when his confession turned into a judgment of them. They gave him a standing ovation.

Again, the lesson of the story lies deeper than the fact that he was vulnerable and had an affair. The tragedy was in his refusal to acknowledge what was wrong, and in the way this denial hardened into a feigned innocence that led him to blame his congregation. In the end he blamed everyone but the culprit. Today he is selling real estate.

Why didn't he face the truth and himself in good time? If we knew the answer to that, we could be sure of behaving differently ourselves. But we can't. Not to face the truth is the height of irrationality, but we are all the same. It's bad enough when nonbelievers refuse to face themselves. But when believers do, they can use even God to help them cover their tracks.

In the final analysis, those who don't believe are only marginally more open. For while they may admit that they hate themselves, suffer from low self-esteem or whatever, only rarely do they acknowledge that they are responsible for their problems. Once again we see that we share a common humanity. All of us are selfish, but all of us are prone to deny that we are. Seeing that was a critical step in my own journey. For different reasons and by all sorts of mechanisms, we seek to distance ourselves from the painful truth.

How does the lie that we are OK get in the way of our pursuit of happiness and love? It blocks true intimacy in relationships, be they romantic, familial or platonic. We can have no relationship of depth or authenticity if we insist there is nothing wrong with us or that it is always the other person's fault. Our flaws make sustaining good relationships hard enough. But to refuse to take responsibility and admit our flaws makes the intimacy and love we seek in relationships an impossibility. We little realize that the truth that under one set of circumstances is painful becomes liberating under another.

3

The Lie That
We're in Charge

Though you are a man and no god,
you try to think the thoughts of a god.
EZEKIEL, EIGHTH CENTURY B.C.

Why is our inner landscape so foreign to us? It has become forbidden territory because we do not want to face the truth of what is there. If we peel back the layers of denial even a little bit, we may feel, "With friends like Camus, who needs enemies?" It helps to remember what Thomas Hardy said: in effect, if there is a path to the happiness and freedom for which we long, it lies in taking a full look at the worst first (see the epigraph of chapter two). That really is the secret: the worst first. Only when we acknowledge that something is wrong will we start to look for genuine solutions.

But there is something else that will spur on our inner pilgrimage. We cannot shake our conviction that we are made for something more; that there is something we are missing. In our pursuit of happiness we long to be taken outside of ourselves; we want to participate in something larger than self. Here once again, Clamence is an invaluable guide.[1]

Clamence has been on a remarkable inner journey. When the story begins, he feels superior, confident, in charge, and assumes he is the author of his own script. Clamence simply takes it for granted that he is "the master of the universe." He is a thoroughly modern man with confidence in himself and the powers of his reason. There is almost no problem that he cannot solve. Should such a problem arise, education or social action can be trusted to take care of it. Arrogant? Well, just a bit. But this man doesn't know what it is to be a loser. He is independent, powerful, respected, wealthy and successful in all the areas that matter to him—in business, with women and in society. So who needs God when you virtually are one? As Bertrand Russell said, "Everyone would like to be God, if it were possible; some . . . find it difficult to admit the impossibility."[2]

But that insight is precisely the measure of the distance Clamence has to journey. He has to travel slowly from believing that he is God to admitting the utter impossibility. For years Clamence had congratulated himself on his good looks, good health and easy conscience. But his understanding of himself changes beyond recall when he realizes he is finite, dependent, insecure and—worse still—flawed. That is a long distance to travel by anybody's measurement.

What gets Clamence going on the search is his honesty, not some stupid blunder he's been trapped by. He had not invested his money unwisely, been caught in a shady business deal or tumbled into bed with a trusted friend's wife. What he had done he had done alone, in the dark; no one had seen or would ever need to know. Yet that secret would haunt him, totally and unalterably changing his self-understanding; and it would open up an unexplored inner world of doubt, insecurities and flaws. From the moment he fails to try to save the woman on the bridge, a corner is turned, a door closed. Life will never again be comfortable. Once he has taken a glimpse into his own subterranean depths, there can be no going back. He has looked in the mirror, and the reflection looking back at him is anything but innocent.

Unexpected Insecurity

Clamence's fascinating inner journey reveals three levels of self-understanding through which many pass. At the first level, he is carelessly unaware that anything is wrong because he lives on the surface. That is where most of us start, and some people stay there for a lifetime. In his ignorance and arrogance, typical of this level, Clamence refuses to acknowledge his limits. He thinks he is self-sufficient and recognizes no weaknesses in himself, only in others. He is, in a word, proud. But at least he believes there are good reasons for his pride. He has nothing but contempt for the losers, the weaklings, the failures. He would be in total sympathy with Nietzsche's "Overman." The only function of the weak is to serve as objects for his patronizing disdain.

At the second level of awareness, Clamence catches sight of the first deeper truths about himself. He becomes aware that he is grandiose, self-centered, attention seeking and always trying to control others. He comes up against the fact that he has selfish, ulterior motives for everything he does. He sees, too, that he is finite. He cannot overcome the problem of his nature by sheer force of will. Indeed he is powerless to transform and redirect his nature at all.

Clamence's third level of awareness reveals an even deeper layer of human nature. For at the edges of the newly enlightened circle of his self-understanding, he begins to see what he had been terrified to face: All along he has had a fundamental insecurity that he was seeking to obscure. After he lets down his guard and begins to face his faults, he realizes that even in his puffed-up days of glory there was a dimly recognized weakness from which he was running away. For the first time in his life, it dawns on him why he is so driven.

Following the tortuous honesty of Clamence's journey, the reader begins to see behind his restless pursuit of wealth, professional achievement and sexual conquests: Clamence was in flight from a darkly conscious realization of his insecurity. For if he were truly secure, why did he need to exalt himself larger than life-size? Why did he feel he had to stand out from everyone else? Why did everything about him have to be bigger and better? Clamence knew he was competent professionally. He knew he was far more successful than most. He knew he was very intelligent. To say that was not egotism on his part—it was the truth. Yet he also knew an underlying insecurity even deeper than his giftedness, a basic insecurity that he had never had the courage to face.

At this third level the pervasiveness of insecurity becomes clear. Even when things are going our way and there seems to be no reason for self-doubt, our ceaseless efforts to prove we are *somebody* betray our hidden fears. We feel anxious that someone might discover our pretenses and will find out that we aren't what we appear.

It is a remarkable thought that only the human species spends so much money and time pretending it is other than it really is. The human species is the only form of life that feels insecure. For as G. K. Chesterton remarked, "Who has ever found an anthill decorated with statues of celebrated ants? Who has seen a beehive carved up with the images of gorgeous queens of old?"[3] Dogs do not put on airs because they are larger than squirrels. Nor do they become depressed because they are not as big as gorillas. Animals are content to be what they are.

But that is no credit of theirs. The fact is, animals cannot imagine any other form than the one they have been given. They cannot, as we can, reach beyond their limits and pretend to be bigger or better—younger or older, more gifted or beautiful—than they are. Animals, in this sense, are lucky. They don't walk around feeling incomplete and insecure. Our human imagination, however, is a double-edged sword. It enables us to anticipate the future, recall the past, turn all the universe into our here and now. But it is also what allows us to think our self-exalting thoughts and refuse to be content with what we are.

The Terror of Insecurity

One way we seek to overcome our insecurity is through asserting power. Whether over people, land, possessions, bank accounts, positions or data, we relentlessly try to assert our dominion and so to prove our worth. "Of the infinite desires of man," wrote Bertrand Russell, "the chief are the desires for power and glory."

Why is this so? Are such desires prompted simply by our pride and vanity? That is surely part of it. But at a deeper level they are integrally connected to our insecurity. Reinhold Niebuhr writes, "The school of modern psychology which regards the will to power as the most dominant of human motives has not yet recognized how basically it is related to insecurity."[4] He is right. Those who glory in the will to power are indulging in self-flattery. Beneath such drives is an insecurity that terrifies us. So we use every available means to assert ourselves in order to assuage our sense of weakness. The drive to dominate is to shield ourselves from the drafts blowing up from the abyss of our insecurity.

This understanding goes to the heart of the human predicament. The human ego, as Niebuhr says, "does not feel secure and therefore grasps for more power in order to make itself secure. It does not regard itself as sufficiently significant or respected or feared, and therefore seeks to enhance its position in nature and in society."

Take a long look into the depths of human insecurity, and you will see that we use cures and self-help formulas to overcome inadequacy and lack of recognition. We pull ourselves up to escape the downward pull of our insecurity. But our strategies for covering over our insecurity serve only to deceive us. They are an illusion, a web of unreality. They may work for a while, but in the end they make us more insecure because we know they are illusory. What is remarkable is the energy we expend to perpetuate what in our hearts we know to be a lie.

The lie of all lies at the heart of this problem is that we keep acting like God when we are only human. We pretend to be infinite and eternal when we are pathetically bound by space and time. Psychotherapist Ernest Becker laments, "Man is driven away from himself, from self-knowledge, self-reflection. He is driven toward things that support the lie of his character."[5] Wilhelm Reich stresses the same point: "What is the dynamic of human misery on this planet? It all stems from man trying to be other than he is."[6] Centuries ago the prophet Ezekiel had made the same point even more tellingly: "Though you are a man and no god, / you try to think the thoughts of a god" (Ezekiel 28:2 NEB).

A while ago I attended two large social events, one of them cultural and one religious. I was struck by how similar they were in certain respects. For example, when people at the cultural affair were introducing themselves, I was amused at how many hints I was given as to why they were important.

And the "bigger" they talked, the more they revealed of their underlying sense of inadequacy. Later, at the religious gathering, I met a man who told me in the first three minutes how humbled he was to see "how the Lord has really blessed [his] ministry." Which, it turned out, meant that his books and videos were selling spectacularly well. To give him the benefit of the doubt, I want to take that at face value. But less ambiguous were all the pastors I met who described their churches first by their sizes, almost as if they were successful business franchises.

Why do we all tend to behave like that, regardless of the occasion? Whether it is a congressman vying for the best table in the restaurant so that he can be seen, or a minister informing us of how many copies of his books have sold, or a neighbor down the street who is a notorious name-dropper, the root of the problem is the same. Insecurity gives us a constant need to go beyond ourselves for affirmation.

Although we see our insecurity when we compare ourselves to the animal kingdom, we can also see our greatness. As Chesterton points out:

> The fact that apes have hands is far less interesting to the philosopher than the fact that having hands he does next to nothing with them; does not play knuckle-bones or the violin; does not carve marble or carve mutton. People talk of barbaric architecture and debased art. But elephants do not build colossal temples of ivory even in a rococo style; camels do not paint even bad pictures, though equipped with the material of many camel's hair brushes.

So while it is true that we are insecure, we also *know* that we are. And in the gap between what we experience and what we long for is a hint, an intuition and a signal of some truth beyond. As the French mathematician and philosopher Blaise Pascal argued, "The greatness of man is so evident that it is even proved by his wretchedness. For what in animals is called nature we call wretchedness in man; by which we recognize that, his nature now being like that of animals, has fallen from a better nature which once was his. For who is unhappy at not being a king except a deposed king?"[7]

The Claim to the Right to Myself
What happens when our strategies of denial are detected and our defenses

have broken down? Camus's honesty at this point of his own unmasking is stunning. Clamence continues: "I was always bursting with vanity. I, I, I, is the refrain of my whole life, which could be heard in everything I said. . . . I would pretend to get excited about some cause foreign to my daily life . . . but everything slid off—yes, just rolled off me. I never remembered anything but myself."

We are proud and self-centered. What is foremost in each of our minds is *my* agenda, *my* concerns. To be sure, we want to be nice because we want everyone to admire and like us. But to discover what our course of action will be, just determine what we think lies in our own best interest. That is what we'll choose. That is what we'll do. Underneath everything, each of us asserts the claim to the right to "myself."

During his period of denial, Clamence believed his own press releases. He saw himself as a magnanimous guy, the kind who'd take the shirt off his back for anyone. And he would have, so long as things went his way. After all, as C. S. Lewis notes wryly, "Everyone feels benevolent if nothing happens to be annoying him at the moment."[8] But the moment Clamence was crossed, he became petty, vindictive, mean-spirited and angry. He greatly admired the traits of loyalty, integrity and sincerity, and felt he possessed them. Yet he would sacrifice principle for pleasure with astonishing speed. Thus he could lie to lovers and keep multiple relationships going without a serious qualm.

Nothing kept Clamence from believing the best about himself. No matter how much evidence to the contrary, he never doubted that his heart was in the right place. Of course it helped greatly that he never looked back, never asked what went wrong, and that he avoided serious reflection of the painful sort. With these and other sleights of hand he was able to feel superior to most and live with no regrets—until the incident on the bridge.

Aren't we all, like Clamence, "great lovers of our own person"? Even children have the desire to stand out from the rest. One young woman told me of her return visit to a kindergarten where she'd taught. There isn't a child on the planet who, knowing Staycee, does not love her. All the children were ecstatic to see her again. But one little boy suddenly piped up and announced to his class, "Yeah, but don't forget, everybody, *I'm* the one she knows best."

There it was. He expressed what is in the heart of us all—the desire to stand out, to be *the one*. As endearing as his comment was, the truth is we find it hard not to want to be exceptional.

Years ago I went to a Christmas party for three-year-olds at my daughter's preschool. It was something to behold, all these freshly scrubbed cherubic faces beaming innocently as they sang Christmas carols. Then it was time for presents and cookies. Pandemonium struck. "Where's my present?" "Her cookie is bigger than mine!" "He got more cake than I did!" "She got to open her present first." Each face bore an expression of three-year-old anguish that someone might get a larger slice of cake or get to the punchbowl first. Deprivation was hardly the issue. There wasn't a child present who did not look well fed and loved. But you would never have guessed that from their behavior. There was no mistaking the signs: They were unabashedly out for number one.

Pride in adult form is better disguised but less appealing. We see it in our attempts to manipulate and control. We see it in the political policies of larger countries dealing with smaller countries, or in chauvinism toward women, or in trying to control our children so they will become the kind of people we think they should be. And we see it in the church just as we see it in the world outside. The real scandal of the televangelists was the vaunting pride and self-absorption that issued in manipulating the lives and hopes of others.

"Everybody" Includes Me

Believe me, I realize I am not immune. I am a public speaker, which is a profession that provides incredible blessings. I never cease to be encouraged by the love and generosity of the people I meet around the country. But there are also dangers. I am usually with a group for only a day or two, during which I can talk to my heart's content without interruption and get paid for it! I receive lots of attention, admiration and genuine affection. I usually receive only positive feedback, perhaps because the critics feel they only have to endure me for a day, so why bother taking exception? I am at my best and most people are warmly responsive. Besides, most people come to conferences expecting their lives to be changed, so I tend to hear extraordinary things about the helpfulness of my contribution, things that most people might hear only a few times in their lives.

I don't want to suggest there aren't enormous demands on a public speaker—more, in fact, than people might suspect; but the rewards are rich and beguiling. I come away with a feeling of security, identity and significance. I fly home having been told that I am wonderful, I am gifted, I am loved. Would I mind signing a few more books? Of course the real test comes when I walk into my home. It tests what I say publicly and who I am privately, because there is no one applauding me as I drive car pool, chauffeur children to endless basketball games and flute lessons, and cook dinner.

Where are the reality checks in a life like that? They certainly don't come when I am on the road. They have to come from the people who know me best. Early on a friend asked, "Becky, do I sense a bit of resistance in you when I tell you my criticisms?" The sad truth is, there *was* a niggle of resentment in me. In my own clever way, I doubtless made it clear that she should take an opinion poll of the last conference I addressed if she intended to point out my flaws.

But something changed. Slowly I started to see that my claim to be "innocent of all charges" was ridiculous. I began to listen and to try to understand. It was a great temptation to go where I only heard the things I wanted to about myself. But slowly I started acknowledging my own faults. I began to deal with the root problems in my life and not merely the symptoms. I saw that my pride and self-centeredness ran deep, far deeper than I had ever imagined.

And I made an amazing discovery. The more I faced myself—my self-deceptions, pockets of unbelief, false confidence, controlling devices and so on—the more I found freedom. It sounds crazy, but the process of naming the problem, owning it as mine, working on it, has led to an enormous surge forward in my pilgrimage. I have come to see that I will never do anything for one reason. The heart is indeed deceitful above all things. There is always the snare of self and always the possibility of some self-serving dimension in everything I do. But that has not buried me in despair. The paradox is that the clearer I am about what is wrong, the more open I become to seeking solutions. And the clearer I am about the human heart, the more I can take praise with a heavy dose of salt.

In the Cosmic Driver's Seat

There is another self-exalting lie that is integrally associated with pride: the myth that we control our own lives, that we are in charge. Becker again nails the fallacy:

> We don't want to admit that we are fundamentally dishonest about reality, that we really do not control our own lives. We don't want to admit that we do not stand alone, that we always rely on something that transcends us, some system of ideas and powers in which we are imbedded and which supports us. The power is not always obvious . . . but it keeps a person buoyed up in ignorance . . . of the fact he does not rest on his own center.

The point is so obvious that a moment's thought would show its truth. We would dismiss as mad anyone who announced that he or she was God. Yet we still act as if we were, or at least as if we were entirely autonomous. And we Americans have our own national reasons for going along with this delusion. We prize "rugged individualism." We pride ourselves on being self-made people who have succeeded without favors from anyone.

Of course we need short memories and even shorter sight to convince ourselves of such an absurdity. Apart from the rare mountain hermits, we all depend on other people, yet most of the time we seem to pull off the illusion with aplomb. The really amazing thing is how long it takes us to realize we are not God, that over the deepest things in life we are not in the driver's seat of the universe.

Most parents would sacrifice anything to help their child in trouble. Beyond a few short years, however, even our children's lives are lived outside the realm of our control. Even when they're small, we cannot be with them every second. We cannot make their choices or protect them from the choices of others.

Before I had children, I traveled a great deal more. And one refrain I heard repeatedly was of successful professionals who were having trouble with their children. I remember one incident vividly. With the president of a West Coast think tank, the physicist I mentioned in chapter one, I discussed several intriguing issues before he asked me what I did professionally. When I told him, a look of amazement spread over his face. "But—but you *seemed* like such a *thinking* person," he said. I laughed and reminded him that faith and reason are not mutually exclusive.

By the look on his face, I knew I should have added "sanity." He quickly recovered and said, "I'm a scientist, you know, a rational person. I've never seen much need for God. All my life I've felt in charge and in control. I've been extremely successful and made it to the top. If there's a problem at work, I call a meeting or write a note to my secretary and it is quickly resolved.

"Yet nothing is simple or easily resolved at home. My children don't relate to me easily. They don't listen to me or do what I say. They accuse me of trying to control their lives. When I walk into the same room as my son, he starts to stammer. What hurts is that they can't seem to appreciate how much I care and that I'm doing all of this for them.

"But I'll tell you one lesson I've learned. I always said I don't believe in God—but I've acted like one. I thought that since I had my children's best interests at heart, they'd be glad for my direction. I thought I could influence them, but I can't. My children have taught me the hardest lesson of my life—that I'm not in control over what matters to me most. It's funny, but it's now when I see I'm not God that I see I need some help. The question of whether there is a God has finally started to matter."

I have heard countless variations of this story. And the more professionally successful the parents, the harder they find it to learn the lesson.

Many years ago I had some minor surgery. Never having had an operation, I fully expected that an hour or so afterward I would walk out of the hospital, briefcase in hand, and be home for lunch. Just before I began getting the anesthetic, I started telling the surgeon a funny incident that happened on the way to the hospital. He and the rest of the operating-room staff became involved in the story and were eager for me to get to the punch line before the drug took effect. Sure enough, just as I got to the funny part, the drug hit me. I couldn't believe its force. As I started to close my eyes, everyone stationed around the operating table was shouting,

"Becky, come on! Finish the story!" It felt at the time like the hardest thing I had ever done to get out the final two words. But I did it. And I went under to the sound of raucous laughter.

I learned something from that experience. It took the entire day to get out from under the effects of the drug. I did not dance out of the recovery room, grab my briefcase and start dictating. The reality was, I could not even tell the recovery nurse coherently whether I wanted a 7-Up or a cola. I was struck by how terribly vulnerable I was. I had arrived full of my sense of schedule, my plans and how I was going to run my day. I grandly thought I'd be home in hours. But all it took was a few chemicals in my system, and I was out of commission and anything but in control.

Why was the scientist taken aback by his inability to control his children and I by the power of the anesthetic? Because we both overestimated our capacity to be in charge. Our finiteness caught up with us; our limits had the last word.

Seeing It Like It Isn't

It's embarrassing to make such poor judgments about our capabilities. Why do we do it? The answer is fascinating because it contains the secret of both human greatness and weakness. Our imagination, which is the most powerful faculty we have, gives us the capacity to think that we are other than we are—to daydream that we are stronger, richer, more successful and in some other place than we are in fact. In short, our imagination gives us an almost infinite capacity to transcend our limits—at least in our heads.

This godlike gift is the secret of human genius. It lies behind our art, music and business enterprise. But it is also the reason for the dark genius of our evil and the empty delusions of our folly. We can imagine the impossible even when we cannot pull it off. We think we are calm and cool under pressure, or understanding and sympathetic to others, or always full of goodwill to the world. Yet when those qualities are tested, the reality may be very different. I always imagined that I was a person of great patience— but then I became a mother. Patience in my head and patience in my experience proved to be two very different things.

The double-edged gift of imagination can inflate our pride and disguise our insecurity. Our best can always be better and our worst not quite so bad. All too human, we can act the part of God. Patently flawed, we can pass ourselves off as paragons of virtue. And we can usually sustain our feeble illusion until life makes that deception impossible—fortunately.

Confusing ourselves with God? Some people are offended to think they do anything so ludicrous. But the delusions that result from the abuse of imagination are more common than they think. In fact, they are universal and a key to our predicament. The truth is, we hate not being God. "I am nothing and I should be everything," Karl Marx said in his defiant revolutionary declaration. "But man, poor denuded creature, has to build and earn an inner value and security. He must repress his smallness in the adult world, his failure to live up to adult commands and codes. He must repress his own feelings of physical and moral inadequacy—not only the inadequacy of his good intentions but also his guilt and evil intentions."[9]

This "God complex" of ours is vividly portrayed in the Old Testament story of Nebuchadnezzar. When she was younger, my daughter, Elizabeth, who loves a good story, once said as we were settling down for our nightly reading, "Mommy, read me the story about that man who thought he was God one day and then started eating grass the next day."

She'd seen it. Who else could soar on self-exalting thoughts one day and then plummet to such degradation the next? But Nebuchadnezzar's problem was no different from ours. He went beyond us only because his royal power enabled him to experience his folly to the point of madness.

The same God complex is alive and well today, sometimes in equally extraordinary forms. A friend came over the other day very enthusiastic about a New Age seminar she had attended. She said, "I've finally realized there is no bad in me. I can only do good because I am good. God is in everything. Therefore I am God and God is me. I must only think positive thoughts and not let anything negative get in me or get me down. I don't say anything is wrong anymore, I just say, 'It doesn't work for me.'"

"You are the mother of teenagers," I responded. "How does your philosophy work out in raising children? Are they permitted to follow the same logic when you tell them to be in at midnight? 'Sorry, Mom, that just doesn't work for me.'"

She hadn't thought of that. But it stands to reason that a philosophy we would never want our children to adopt can't be much of a philosophy. Her "new" philosophy was just old-fashioned pantheism that sees God and the creation as the same thing. The New Age wrappings may be modern, but it's the same old illusion underneath. Whether it was her folly in believing she was God or mine in believing in my own invincibility under anesthesia, the illusion is the same. We were both suffering from seeing life as it isn't.

I've had to face variations on this God complex in myself time and again, and all the more powerfully since I came to believe in God. It might start from a desire to help a friend or from a concern for someone in crisis. But in no time I slip into thinking that I'm responsible for their well-being, that I can do something to change them or make the situation better, or that I know precisely what is best for them. To simply love a person and help as best I can and commit them to God's care, without trying to intervene and fix things, I find very difficult indeed. This kind of behavior is not untypical of a firstborn child (which I am), and since I am a woman and a believer, the desire to nurture comes naturally. But the problem is more serious than that. Nurture and love are one thing. Playing God in someone's life is another.

This God complex is far more deeply embedded in us than we realize. Even the most mature believers can fall off the wagon when hubris tells them that they are better and more powerful than they really are. I suspect that the desire to be God is one reason the New Age movement took America by storm. It's the creed of our dreams. All you wanted to believe, but were told is wrong, is right. You cannot fail. You are God. So if it works for you, do it, grab it, smoke it, go for it. You owe it to yourself. It's not up to you to worry about the next person. That's their karma.

This is self-absorption masquerading as self-improvement. After all, points out Fred Bruning,

> who has time to work for peace and harmony if he is spending three nights a week doing crystal therapy or life regression? Volunteer at a soup kitchen? Visit the elderly? Press for human rights? Demonstrate for nuclear disarmament? No way. Better to sit cross-legged in a geodesic dome and meditate one's self toward the millennium . . . complete with Tibetan bells, zither

music, crystals, green candles, and Ayurvedic teas at the congress on "harmonic convergence."[10]

Some years ago when Shirley MacLaine announced plans for a three-hundred-acre resort in Colorado with an extensive line of meditation and healing services, she said: "I want this to be all mine. My energy, my control. I want to prove that spirituality is profitable."[11] MacLaine gives credence to the fact that what goes by the name of religion in the modern world is to a great extent unbridled human self-assertion in religious disguise.

Reinhold Niebuhr, the great prophet of realism, put the point bluntly. "Man is ignorant and involved in the limitations of a finite man; but he pretends he is not limited. He assumes he can gradually transcend finite limitations until his mind becomes identical with the universal mind." MacLaine may dub such realism "the old-self-sabotage patterns," but the reality of life bears out far more what the ancient Greeks called *hubris* and the Bible *sin.*

So our insecurity drives us to seek ever more control, to be in charge of ourselves and masters of our universe. And our pride makes us think we are capable of such an absurdity.

Why is it so important that we face our insecurity and pride? Because they prevent us from experiencing the happiness and bliss we seek. To always attempt to take charge diminishes our ability to experience ecstasy. Indeed we soon discover that what we are able to control is usually too small to satisfy us for very long.

A friend was doing everything to entice a man to become interested in her. After he finally called, she was dismissive: "Who wants him if he wasn't strong enough to resist my manipulation? I don't want someone I can control. He can't be that great if he's smitten with me." There it is. Our insecurity fuels our pride and prompts us to take charge, but our control undermines the very bliss we long for.

Anyone for Change?

Camus's Clamence comes down squarely on the side of realism. Whatever his impulses and desires, he has learned from the inside out that he is not God. He is too flawed, too finite, too insecure for such a conceit. But he is still left wanting three things. First, he wants to be rid of his feelings of insignificance, of the sense of his smallness in the universe. He wants to know his life has not been in vain. He wants his wistfulness for a missing something to be satisfied. His life is pleasant enough on the outside, but inside he feels empty and in anguish. He knows the homelessness of the human spirit.

Second, Clamence wants to be rid of his faults. He desires to resolve his guilt, long buried but now out in the open. And finally, he wants to be made better. He wishes to have self-esteem back. He knows he can't live without a sense of worth, but can he now find worth based in reality, not fantasy? For the first time in his life, Clamence is thoroughly and undeniably unhappy with himself.

If Clamence is not happy with the way he is, someone will say, why doesn't he change? Why doesn't he quit bellyaching and do something about it? Why doesn't he tackle and change what he does not like? That, after all, is the American way. We know how to take charge, use our ingenuity, apply a bit of know-how, get a firm grip on the problem and spin out a better product. Maybe, we muse, Clamence's problem is that he is just too French. Europeans get so bogged down with angst, they always end up making things too complex. A cheerful, optimistic American would probably come to Clamence and say, "Look, I see that you're feeling depressed. But I have a wonderful ten-step self-help plan. And if you'll just follow the simple formula, you'll be feeling good about yourself in no time."

Clamence, no doubt, would look at him in wry bemusement: "A self-help book, Monsieur? Have you heard about the well-known benefits of rearranging the deck chairs on the *Titanic?*"

Undaunted, our irrepressible American responds, "You know what your problem is? You need to get your cholesterol down. Start a jogging program. Change your diet. Then you'll stop having all these depressing thoughts."

Clamence answers, "Ah, *mon ami,* what you fail to see is that your cure only reforms my habits. But how does someone reform the heart?"

Clamence would be right. Anyone who faces "the worst first" knows that we cannot even control ourselves. We need a solution from beyond ourselves. The happiness we want is beyond our reach, and everything depends on whether there is the possibility of change. So our journey continues, but realism and its requirements sharpen our sense of direction.

4

Worshiping
the Wrong Things

A life always expresses the result of our dominant thoughts.
SØREN KIERKEGAARD

Take away the life lie from the average man
and you take away his happiness.
HENRIK IBSEN

Playing God is not just difficult, it's impossible. But because of our blind pride, we play God, we seem to have to play God, and we keep on playing God. And because of our finiteness, we just can't quite ever make it. So we have to look elsewhere for a backup, a homemade God substitute. We thus spend our lives swinging between the impossible (playing God) and the inadequate (relying on anything short of God to be God).

At the same time we feel a different sort of pull between two realities in our nature. We soon discover that whatever is wrong with us, we can always point to something else. Alongside our faults, there is another side: something that appears almost Godlike in us. On the one hand, as Ernest

Becker observes, we find "one thing that has always amazed man is his own inner yearning to be good, an excruciatingly warm and melting attraction toward the 'rightness' of beauty, goodness, and perfection."[1] Indeed, we all know that when we fill ourselves with good things—love or beauty, for example—our spirits soar. A beautiful sonata, a breathtaking landscape, a tender conversation with a loved one can stay with us for days. It causes us to expand, to be better than we normally are; it releases what Abraham Lincoln called "the better angels of our nature."

On the other hand, when we fill the void with envy, jealousy, anger or addictive practices, we cater to the darker side of our nature. Our self doesn't expand, it contracts. Our world gets smaller and smaller until we are turned in on ourselves.

It is therefore obvious that if we do not wish to believe in God, there are two strategies we can follow (playing God ourselves or relying on something else to be God) as well as two sides of our nature to which we can appeal in turn. But that is exactly why we seem fated to live restlessly between our insecurity in being human, which spurs us forward in our search for meaning, and the impossibility of our being divine, which casts us back. Little wonder that under such conditions human society seems like a huge idol-making factory and the human story a saga of restlessness without end.

The Restless Search

Where in all this restlessness are we to seek for happiness? Pascal expresses the dilemma: "We have an idea of happiness and cannot reach it. We perceive an image of truth and possess only a lie."[2] We usually set out optimistically to seek happiness through things such as success, wealth, fame, relationships. But then we discover the hitch: The foundations we need for building our happiness need to be big enough for building our lives. Here we run into trouble, because most of the available foundations just won't do, though it is often only after our hopes start to crumble that we discover how inadequate they are.

Take a competitive, aggressive businessman whose life is seemingly meaningful and happy so long as he is ahead, on top. His identity has been wrapped up in profits and successful deals. It is inconceivable to him that life could be any other way. Then his business crashes, and so does his life. Business success is not big enough to build a life on.

There are countless variations on this tale. I have a friend, a lovely model, whose life is centered in her beauty. She once told me, "The only bargaining chip I have is my looks. If that goes there is nothing left." But can beauty buy happiness? What happens if she gets what she wants and still is not content? What will she do if she loses her beauty when she gets old? Or sick? Another friend tied her happiness to her lover. When he moved on to someone else, she was devastated and her life crumbled.

We need thus to ask ourselves, What are we banking on for our happiness, and what would happen if it were taken away? If high income, physical beauty, the symbols of ease and the right mate are what life is ultimately about, then these ought to be able to sustain us through crisis. But clearly they cannot. These things are not wrong in themselves, but they were never intended to be the foundation on which we build. They are instead the furnishings. The irony is that when these securities fail and our life falls apart, we don't stop to ask, Then what is big enough to build my life upon? Instead, we tend to say, That just proves that there is no God, or my life wouldn't be this miserable. It rarely occurs to us that our lives may be miserable precisely because we have not trusted the one source of security we were meant to build on.

Nonetheless, if it is happiness we are after, where does the modern person go to find it? Once again Clamence illuminates our own longing for fulfillment, as we watch him in his pursuit of happiness. Clamence slowly comes to see that he is in search of what the poet Wallace Stevens calls "an imperishable bliss." In fact, he likens this longing for bliss to worship, only in his case it is worship of himself: "I was bursting with the longing to be immortal. Wasn't this the key to my nature and also a result of the great self-love I have told you about?"[3]

Clamence is saying that human nature and human aspirations point beyond themselves. They cry out for us to lose ourselves in an exalted abandon to something larger than we are. Only that way—yielding everything and holding back nothing—can our deepest needs for love, meaning and security be met. In short, we have a worshiping nature, and until we find the person or object worthy of that commitment we will always be less than we might be—and we know it.

Camus is not the only secular voice to recognize that human aspirations point beyond themselves. Peter Shaffer's brilliant play Equus also explores the subject of worship.[4] The story, about a boy who believes that horses are God, revolves around his relationship to the psychiatrist assigned to his case, Martin Dysart. What intrigues Dysart is not the boy's psychological disorder but the impact his worship has on the way he approaches life. The boy's belief in his god (albeit a horse) has enabled him to relinquish control and surrender himself totally to the object of his worship. And his ability to pray, to love, to surrender himself in worship with reckless abandon makes him pulsate with life and energy. Far from making him dour and passionless ("religious," as most think of it), his worshiping nature has enabled him to live totally involved, experiencing life with his whole being. He knows awe. He is passionate. Far from deadening him, worship has set him on fire! The only problem is that the object of his worship is horses, and that makes him certifiably crazy.

Dysart, on the other hand, is sane. But his sophisticated and clinical approach to life is devoid of all passion. Both physically and spiritually he is sterile. He doesn't know what it means to relinquish control and surrender to something greater than himself. He lives, as he has been trained, to be in control at all times. He looks at the boy's vitality and says, "That boy has known a passion more ferocious than I have felt in any second of my life. And let me tell you something: I envy it. . . . I'm jealous. . . . That's what his stare has been saying to me all the time. 'At least I galloped. When did you?' . . . Passion, you see, can be destroyed by a doctor. It cannot be created."

Dysart's dilemma as psychiatrist is that in order to make the boy "well" he'll have to take away the very thing that gives him life: his worship. "Can you think of anything worse that one can do for anybody than take away their worship?" Dysart asks quietly, contemplating this paradox.

So what is the cure to be? To become as bored, faithless, sterile and "sane" as everyone else? What can the boy expect life to look like when he has been cured and lost his ability to worship? Dysart describes himself and asks if this is an enviable cure for anyone:

> I tell everyone Margaret's the puritan. I'm the pagan. Some pagan! Such wild returns I make to the womb of civilization. Three weeks a year in the Peleponnese, every bed booked in advance, every meal paid for by vouchers, cautious jaunts in hired Fiats, suitcase crammed with Kaopectate! Such a fantastic surrender to the primitive. And I use that word endlessly: "primitive." "Oh, the primitive world," I say. "What instinctual truths were lost with it!" And while I sit there, baiting a poor unimaginative woman with the word, that freaky boy tries to conjure the reality! I sit looking at pages of centaurs trampling the soil of Argos—and outside my window he is trying to *become one*, in a Hampshire field! . . . I watch that woman knitting, night after night—a woman I haven't *kissed* in six years—and he stands in the dark for an hour, sucking the sweat off his God's hairy cheek! (*pause*) Then in the morning, I put away my books on the cultural shelf, close up the Kodachrome snaps of Mount Olympus, touch my reproductive statue of Dionysus for luck—and go off to the hospital to treat him for insanity. Do you see?

Equus is a remarkable play for our time. God is dead, some voices in our culture insist emphatically. But then what is humankind if we are no greater than our focus of worship and all that is left to worship is too small? Like a tongue probing a decaying tooth, Shaffer will not let complacence pass. Unfashionable as it sounds, it is worship, he says, that sets us apart, that makes us unique. To be human is to have to worship. "Real worship! Without worship you shrink. It's as brutal as that." Dysart's frigid skepticism prevents him from embracing faith himself. But his life is irrevocably changed by his encounter with the boy, for now he realizes what has been missing from his own life. He himself was to blame. "I shrank my *own* life. No one can do it for you. I settled for being pallid and provincial, out of my own eternal timidity." To worship horses may be crazy. But misguided devotion may be closer to the truth (and to human greatness) than no devotion at all.

But where do we go to find trustworthy objects for our devotion? Therein lies the problem. Most of us don't attach ourselves to horses. According to Clamence, there are two places people go first in order to fill

the void: a quest for the romantic ideal and, when that fails, for sexual fulfillment. Let's examine such common pursuits of happiness.

Romance

Clamence sees evidence of his worshiping nature in his quest for love. He
wanted to discover the love of his life, the romantic ideal who would solve
all his problems, provide meaning and purpose to his life, and be an object
he could devote himself to forever. Why? Because he recognized how deep
was his need for love. So "inasmuch as I needed to love and be loved I
thought I was in love." He never found his true love, because he could
never make his fantasy fit the reality of the other person. No matter how
ardent his passion, his attachment to himself kept getting in the way. "For
more than thirty years I have been in love exclusively with myself. What
hope was there of losing such a habit?" Furthermore, he couldn't sustain
his interest in the same woman for very long. Finally, love didn't change
him inwardly as he had hoped. He wanted to lose himself in love. But no
matter how electric the initial encounter, once the love dust settled he was
still the same man.

What's going on? What is it that Clamence longs for and can't find? Why
is it that in spite of age, education, intelligence and status, humans have
always played love's fool and thrown caution to the winds? Because the
human spirit hankers after something more. As the poet Wallace Stevens
writes, "But in contentment I still feel the need of some imperishable
bliss."[5] And falling in love surely offers bliss—the almost mystical initial
sense of oneness, of fusion, of understanding, of being taken out of one's
self. Which is why our behavior almost always improves while we are in
this state. We are so in love we are "beside ourselves," not in ourselves.

But as wonderful as it is, it does not seem to solve the problem of our
nature in a permanent way. Eventually we discover we are still the same
person with the same set of flaws. But the fact that we gravitate toward it,
seem so hungry for it, tells us something about how we are made. We have
an inner emptiness longing to be filled.

Clamence's search for his romantic ideal mirrors the yearnings we all
have. Some of us feel it more than others, but hunger and deep desires are

a part of us all. Clamence expresses the human tendency to direct our need toward another person and attach ourselves to that person as the object of our love. This is especially where the modern person, who no longer believes in God, usually starts. We hope, as Clamence did, that finding the romantic ideal will be the answer. As Becker says, "The self-glorification we need in our innermost nature we now look for in the love partner. The love partner becomes the divine ideal within which to fulfill one's life."

What is the logic of this quest? If we are limited and cannot make ourselves better, the reasoning goes, then maybe someone else can. But alas, the search is doomed. Love partners prove to be mortal and needy too. They cannot give a complete and lasting solution to our lack, nor we to theirs. In the end we do not want to lose ourselves forever in someone else. Nor can we bear the strain of forever playing God in a relationship. We simply don't possess the resources.

This is Dick's shattering lesson as he tries to save Nicole in F. Scott Fitzgerald's *Tender Is the Night*. He has always thought of himself as "Lucky Dick" whose charm and goodwill can conquer anything—even Nicole's illness. But by the end of the book he tells her, "I can't do anything for you any more. I'm trying to save myself."[6]

Romantic love can be real, deep and lasting—but only if it is not asked to be what it isn't. It is not within our power to give each other absolution. We are unable to fill every inner crevice of longing in someone else. The fundamental change that people are after is beyond us. The best of love partners finally disappoint us in the same way we disappoint ourselves if we forget that they are as limited and finite as we are.

My agnostic friend whom I mentioned in the first chapter was suffering through the trauma of having been jilted by her lover. She thought she had found the love of all loves, but it failed. She told me: "It didn't fail because I took my relationship with him too lightly. Rather, I asked too much of it. I thought that once I found the right person to love, everything else would fall into place. And for a while it did. I thought love had finally conquered my lifelong problems with anger and distrust. I decided I had exaggerated the underside of myself. I had nasty, spiteful bits, to be sure, but essentially I was good. That, I thought, was love's lesson to me.

"Eventually, however, my dark side reared its head again. I hadn't changed as much as I had hoped. When my old problems emerged, he began to back away. So I started clinging more, demanding more. All my fears and anxieties that he wouldn't love me, that he'd reject me for someone else, kept edging into the relationship. I banked all my need for love in him and told him so. He said he couldn't bear the weight of it. I longed for him to solve all my problems, meet all my needs. I wanted him to give ultimate meaning and purpose to my life so I wouldn't be left alone. He told me no one could sustain the pressure of being a god for someone else.

"I feel like I'm made to run on the fuel of love, but the minute I get in a relationship I start to make him my center, my god, and the relationship crumbles. So I'm alone again, wondering why my immense wish to be loved can't be gratified. Why do we carry such a hunger when it can never be met? It all feels like a sick joke."

She concluded, like Clamence, that the sooner she abandoned her child-like longing to be loved, the better off she would be. She wanted to call her need for love "a sick joke," but I told her she had it right. She *is* made to run on the fuel of love.

She said she foolishly thought love would heal her and make her better. I told her she was right again. But human love by itself will never be able to handle the immensity of the task. It can go away or die or fail us at the precise moment we need it most. And if it is to meet our needs and longings, love itself must have a base. What amazed me was that she never wondered whether her longing for love might actually be valid and perhaps she had simply banked her desperate need for it in the wrong place.

Sexuality
When the romantic ideal failed, Clamence continued his search to fill the inner void by turning to sexuality. He now turned deliberately from one extreme to the other. Before he had wanted too much from the one he loved. Now he wanted too little. Where he had failed at first to "find himself" in romantic love, he now attempted to "lose himself" in casual sex. He descended from the angelic to the animal and denied himself nothing.

But does it work any better? Clamence is too frank, and free love is too shallow, to allow him to fool himself. The pursuit of happiness through sexuality led him eventually to debauchery, but long before then he discovered the best and worst of easy sex. "In it you possess only yourself; hence it remains the favorite pastime of the great lovers of their own person." Happiness is no more attained through sexuality than through romantic love. Besides, age is especially cruel to hedonism. "One plays at being immortal and after a few weeks one does not know whether or not one can hang on till the next day."

The one thing Clamence does gain from his sexual conquests, at least for a while, is a way of escape, a chance to help him forget. His debauchery is like living in a fog with dulled senses, but that is just what he wants. It enables him to forget his unhappiness, his ache. He knows that the empty bottles in his room, like the empty affairs in his life, are symbols of what he has become. They are the badges of his existence, just as for John Cheever's Mr. Lawton they are "the buttonless shirt, the vouchers and bank statements, the order blanks, and the empty glass."[7] They symbolize a terrible emptiness in Clamence's life, but at least his "cure" has dulled and quieted his despair.

But even the narcotic of debauchery does not last. One day on an ocean liner Clamence sees a black speck on the water, and his heart begins to pound wildly. At once he thinks of the drowning woman he had failed to save. At that moment he knows that her cry for help has never left him. He will never be able to distance himself from the discovery of his "other self." The knowledge of who he is "would continue to await me on seas and rivers, everywhere, in short, where lies the bitter waters of baptism . . . I had to submit and admit my guilt."

I have a Christian friend, a single woman, who has been trying to get out of a long-term affair with a married man. One only needs to hear ten minutes of the story of her life to understand why she is so vulnerable. She too was seeking love. But while my first friend was looking for someone else to worship, this woman seems to want to be worshiped herself. She wanted to know there was a man who couldn't live without her, who wanted her at any price, whose first and last thoughts each day were about her. "I *want* him to be addicted to me," she says in sad desperation.

This woman's search for love ended in a serious sexual addiction. She knew that what she was doing violated everything she believed in. She knew the man was deeply troubled. She knew he treated her badly, and in her heart she knew she didn't respect him. And she hated herself for what she was doing. Again and again she promised herself she would break it off. But after a while the hunger intensified, and she would break down and call him. By the time this woman came into my life, she wasn't sure she wanted to live.

Self-Help

Clamence's quests for happiness through romance and sexuality were both catastrophic failures. They only left him more aware of his problem and deeper in his aloneness. In his feverish pursuit, he hoped that his problems would somehow disappear, but he discovers that happiness cannot last or solve anything if it is used as a means to hide from one's problem. The reality of his deeper problem always awaits him, and he knows there will be no happiness unless the problem is faced.

Clamence's next step is to seek to *understand his condition* or, as we would say a generation later, to seek help by turning to psychological self-scrutiny. Clamence looks deep within himself, and he gives us a characteristically illuminating account of what it means to be human. But mere knowledge can neither liberate nor change him. He recognizes that he is guilty beyond a shadow of a doubt. But important as self-reflection and analysis are, they cannot absolve him or take the burden from his conscience.

So many today put such confidence in the mystique of psychology that they are not likely to follow Clamence easily in recognizing that self-help is inadequate. We need to remember that there are two perils in psychological self-scrutiny. One is the assumption that we can conquer all our problems through insight and self-awareness. The underlying premise is that if we analyze our problems correctly, we can overcome them. We think that to *understand* how our flaws have developed will mean we have power over them. We assume that if we *see* how a thing works and see what has gone wrong, then all we need to do is take charge of the problem (in this case our own nature) and correct it. The modern psychological assumption is that if we discover our motives and can be shown why we feel guilty or unhappy, then we will be able to accept ourselves and be content.

Talk about a leap of faith! A moment's thought would show that important as self-awareness is, it only enlightens us about the nature of our problems; it doesn't solve or heal them, and the best practitioners make no claims for anything else. Robert Coles, the eminent Harvard psychiatrist, once told his class, partly in jest, partly mocking the efficacy of his profession, about a man who had gone to a psychoanalyst for fifteen years. "I went because I was so hostile and mean-spirited," the man said. "I'm just as hostile and mean-spirited as I ever was—only now I know *why* I'm so nasty!"[8]

The second peril lies in the widely accepted notion that guilt feelings are always wrong. It is true that psychology has made a tremendous contribution in helping us recognize "false guilt," those feelings of guilt that are unrelated to any objective wrong. But it is a mistake to then assume that there is no such thing as wrong and guilt *at all*. What happens when the guilt is real and deserved, as Clamence knew it was in his case? How can psychology help us with that?

Ernest Becker, a disciple of Freud who like Freud did not embrace religious faith, is like a voice crying in the psychological wilderness: "Guilt is not a result of infantile fantasy but of self-conscious adult reality. There is no strength that can overcome guilt unless it be the strength of a god."

Realizing that self-awareness is not enough, Clamence goes further and tries the next logical strategy: self-reform. Turning to the grit-your-teeth-and-try-harder approach, he earnestly tries to change his self-seeking ways. He even tries abstinence for a (very) brief stint. But he soon discovers that disciplined efforts at mastering the flesh can only revise outward habits. The problem lies deeper than that.

The problem is not external; it is with the essence of who we are. How do we cure a self-absorbed nature? How do we stop having ulterior motives? What formula do we follow to keep us from being selfish—just try harder? Clamence sees that no effort of his own could enable him to love selflessly. No amount of discipline and self-help treatments could cure his self-centeredness and stubborn pride. After all, what cure is there that would enable him to go "cold turkey" when the cause of the problem, the very thing he is addicted to, is *himself?*

Clamence comes face to face with our inability to heal ourselves. If there is any hope for change, it has to come from outside the individual, from "beyond." Becker says: "All the analysis in the world doesn't allow the person to find out who he is and why he is here on earth. Why he has to die, and how he can make his life a triumph. It is when psychology pretends to do this, when it offers itself as a full explanation of human unhappiness, that it becomes a fraud that makes an impasse from which he cannot escape."

Religion

Romance, sex, self-awareness—these are three of the leading avenues down which modern people hurry in their pursuit of happiness. There are many more, some illicit (such as drugs), some highly respected (such as work). But at a common point, a suspicion begins to nag. Isn't there a common thread running through them all? They all assume that we will find the answer on our own, with no light or strength beyond the human. But maybe that is the problem. Perhaps our answer needs to be *other* than what we have tried thus far. This brings us to religion. After all, throughout all of history humans have turned to religion as the leading agent of change and principal source of happiness. Perhaps religion holds the answer to Clamence's search—and ours.

Not so fast! Religion, as we have seen, can be one of the subtlest forms of denial, and the same caution is needed here. Clamence, however, needs no warnings. As a typical modern man, he shares many of the primitive fears and doubts about God that are common to us all. So for all the urgency of his situation, he resists the notion that God is any answer. Clamence wonders whether his personality might be destroyed if he were to submit to God. What would happen to his identity? And yet. And yet. There is always the thought "But when you don't like your own life, when you know that you must change lives, you don't have any choice, do you? What can one do to become another? Impossible. One would have to cease being anyone, forget oneself for someone else, at least once. But how?"

That is a fair question. What *does* happen to our personality when we surrender to God? Does submission to God mean that self as we know it is obliterated? We have only to think of drink, drugs and workaholism to remember how surrendering ourselves to something usually works against us by entrapping and enslaving us. Who's to say the same thing will not happen if we surrender to God? Isn't it a contradiction to hope that if we submit to God we will find ourselves? How can we grow into full person-hood if we give over our center, our identity, to a higher power?

All of us have known religious people who ruin the thought of religion for anyone else. They fit our worst stereotypes. They seem to plod through life with almost no passion, intelligence or zest, or they speak as if they walk around waiting for direct orders from Above before deciding whether to fix dinner or wash the dishes. They may talk of being "indwelt by God," but one is left wondering what happened to the person who dwelled there previously.

It is a plain fact that some people seem less alive after they "surrender to God" than before—and there is a reason. Religion in general can be one of the worst forms of "bad faith," because we so easily turn to religion to escape the responsibility of our freedom. We do not fully appreciate the challenge of our freedom because it requires so much of us. So we "turn to God" and shrug off all our responsibility on him in the hope that he will override our freedom and, like some great celestial autopilot, give us an error-free ride through life under his control.

I met a woman who was deeply involved in a tight religious commu-nity (or "cult"). Her previous life had been a walk on the wild side. When she started searching for God she considered the Christian faith briefly, but the reason she rejected it was revealing: "I couldn't bear the weight of freedom. I wanted to be told what to eat, to wear, to think. It terrified me that from a Christian perspective, spiritual growth would be dependent on my relationship with a hidden God whom I had to seek in Scripture and prayer, and that I was responsible for my choices. I had so abused my freedom in the past that I couldn't believe in a God who expected me, even with his help, to use my freedom properly this time.

He was asking too much of his creation, this Christian God."

Her argument exactly parallels Ivan's complaint against Christ in Dostoyevsky's *The Brothers Karamazov*. Ivan, who is an atheist, tells his believing brother Alyosha a story about a ninety-year-old cardinal called the Grand Inquisitor who challenges Christ when he returns to earth. The Grand Inquisitor, who is speaking for Ivan, is furious with Christ for giving human beings the freedom to choose. He concludes that we are not smart enough, good enough or brave enough to be entrusted with such freedom: "Nothing has ever been more unsupportable for a man and a human society than freedom. . . . Turn these stones into bread and mankind will run after Thee like a flock of sheep, lest Thou withdraw thy hand and deny them the bread."[9]

According to the Grand Inquisitor, Jesus made it too hard for us when he refused the bread in the wilderness for the bread of heaven. He rebukes Christ by telling him, "Thou wouldst not deprive man of freedom, thinking what is freedom worth if it's bought with bread?" Faith, he concludes, is asking too much of an imperfect people who are "weighed down with the fearful burden of choice."

Certainly our human desire is for Someone to step in and make it all better, Someone to take away all our doubts and fears and pain. We are fearful of the risks in being asked simply to believe in a world of such ambiguity and with lives so constantly threatened at their edges by tragedy and terror. We want God to do something dramatic so that we can know beyond doubt that he is there. Wormwood, the senior devil who writes letters to his earthly emissary in C. S. Lewis's *The Screwtape Letters*, understands well the lure of this longing: "You must have wondered why the enemy [God] does not make more use of His power . . . the irresistible and the indisputable."[10]

The quick-cure resort to religion as a form of bad faith is far too common, so common in fact that many people assume that conversion is only for those too weak to be independent. Faith in God, it is supposed, is a crutch for people in crisis, who turn to outside help because they cannot get by on their own. In Clamence's case, he does consider religion but rejects it with a further twist. It would mean he would have to submit to someone else's authority. And that is intolerable to him. Clamence must be in charge. He must dominate to the end. It may be a lousy life, but at least it is his. Even if he sees in the end that he has tragically failed to grasp the meaning and purpose of life, he will defend to the death his right to be wrong!

The Ultimate Predicament

The key to understanding Camus's novel is to understand Clamence's full name—Jean Baptiste Clamence. Like John the Baptist, Clamence is a prophet in the wilderness, informing us of our sin, telling us we are guilty. True to his last name, he also holds out an offer of clemency—but it is a cynical, caustic forgiveness that he offers. Clamence takes it upon himself to forgive the rest of the world, but only because there is no one left in heaven to do it. And by forgiving the rest of us, he can position himself higher than us and still maintain his conceit of being in control. His calculated confession, which is the only reprieve from guilt he can find, is actually the tool by which he tries to expose our guilt and deflect his own.

At first reading, the powerful honesty of Clamence's confession is moving. Only by the end of the story do we realize the fierceness of his pride, a pride so deep that it will accuse the entire human race rather than repent. It is this arrogance that prompted Simone de Beauvoir to say of Clamence that "from penitent he became judge."[11]

Yet what a hollow victory when winning simply means beating us to the punch with the news of our common guilt. Camus himself provides the most succinct explanation of Clamence and *The Fall:*

> He has a modern heart, which means that he can't stand being judged. Thus he hastens to try himself but he does it so as better to judge others. The mirror into which he looks will finally be held out to others. Where does the confession begin, where the accusation? Is the man who speaks putting himself on trial, or his era? Is he a particular case or the man of the day? A sole truth, in any case, in this studied play of mirrors: pain, and what it promises.[12]

Thus Camus brings us to the final battleground where the human soul stands face to face with its predicament. In a way, our journey finds us knocking at the doors of pride once again. What is the basic human disorder? According to Brazilian psychiatrist Keppe, it is "the disease of theomania—the desire to be god . . . the desire to be the playwright instead of the actor in the drama."[13]

What, then, can we conclude from our survey of different paths to happiness? If the happiness we seek includes victory over human limitations, then it cannot be carried out by ourselves or any other human being. We all share the same problems. We simply cannot draw up such a power from within us. Only what transcends us can transform us.

There is therefore something poignant about our condition. We respond to beauty and we have a longing to worship; yet some fundamental bias leads us to worship what is wrong and pin our hopes forlornly on what can never be adequate. In the search to fill our emptiness, we go outside ourselves for an answer, and our cures prove not to be big enough to build our life upon.

But there, according to Camus, is where we confront our ultimate predicament. Even when we finally see that the solution must come from a source higher and other than ourselves, there remains within us a fierce pride that refuses to submit. Clamence, the thoroughly modern person, fails in his pursuit of happiness because even when he admits his guilt, his pride remains adamant. I may be miserable, he says (and millions with him), but at least I am in charge. I may be forced to face my sin, but never will I weaken to accept grace.

5

Who Can Tell Me
What Is Wrong?

It is in our hearts that the evil lies, and it is from our hearts
that it must be plucked out.
BERTRAND RUSSELL

My sin was all the more incurable
because I did not think myself a sinner.
AUGUSTINE OF HIPPO

Two questions have always fascinated me: If it is happiness we are
after, why are people willing to stay miserable for so long? And what finally
makes someone say, "Enough! I refuse to go on this way. I will do whatever
it takes to change"? A lot of ink has flowed on the subject of change, but in
the final analysis, no one knows for sure why people do—or don't—
change.

It is clear we don't change unless something grabs our attention. The
attention grabber could be anything: a sense of inadequacy or anxiety,
being fed up with feeling angry or worthless, a lack of inner peace, an
empty marriage or frustration with being single, a difficult child, a pay raise

that didn't bring the desired self-satisfaction, the shock of some pattern of behavior getting out of control, getting involved in destructive or unsatis-factory relationships and not knowing why. Whatever the seeds of discon-tent, we finally cross some critical threshold at which we get disgusted or dissatisfied enough to decide to do something about it. We've uncovered a new depth of unhappiness. We can't coast anymore. We are nudged or cat-apulted into beginning a search for an answer.

Our first inclination is to "fix" the problem externally: change spouses, lose weight, switch jobs. But sooner or later, even with the new spouse, new body, new job, we're back to where we started, and that's depressing. Yet even at this stage, the last thing we're prepared to consider is that part of the problem may be ours. Indeed, our difficulty in owning the problem is the deepest part of the problem.

Here is where the self-help movement (and market) steps in. The solu-tion to dissatisfaction with yourself, it says, is the opposite of what most people think. The answer is: Be satisfied with who you are! Love yourself! Believe in yourself! Actualize your potential! Quit listening to all those neg-ative tapes! And by the way, it helps if you can make a lot of money.

But what has this formula produced? A generation of self-actualized, fully realized, daring-to-confront people, who have read all the books and know how to be their own best friend, who own a lot of Internet stock, yet who wonder why they can't make a lasting relationship, why they still feel flickers of doubt and insecurity, why the old patterns seem as ironclad as ever. Clearly our bootstrap remedies have not worked. The problem is at a deeper level than a superficial cure can touch.

Cracking Through Complacency

What I have just described is not the story of anyone in particular, but it fits the experience of many people I know or have met. What's fascinating is how ordinary experience is so close to the unflinching diagnoses of modern observers like Becker and Camus—only they've given it a lot more thought than most of us.

While ours is a "plain person's journey," we have tried to look deeply at who we are as human beings. We have seen that we are flawed even though we try to pretend otherwise. We have seen that we are insecure no matter how sophisticated our masks to hide it. Regardless of how fervently we pursue happiness, it still eludes us. But we have not yet raised the most fundamental question of all: Why is this so? Why are we flawed instead of whole? selfish instead of consistently generous? insecure and neurotic instead of secure and content? Why has there been so much havoc on this planet? We become so accustomed to the way things are or so accepting of the immensity of the problems that we become complacent.

Think how complacent we are while we watch that great American institution: television news. In one sense, it is seldom anything new at all. It is simply a passing photo parade of suffering, injustices, absurdities and cruelties. And nearly all of it has to do with what we do to one another. It is we humans who perpetrate crime, wars, discrimination, brutality, violence, drug trafficking. It is we who abuse one another, whether politely or savagely. The result is a tragic fracturing on every level: in the individual psyche and in personal relationships, in families, and at the national and international levels. Yet we get so accustomed to it that it dulls our senses, and it often takes a jolt to remind us how pathetic the conditions are on this planet.

For me, one jolt came from my children. I was passively watching the evening news, observing people brutally killing one another, blood gushing down their faces, mothers sobbing at their soldier sons' graves. What's the big deal? I went to turn on the potatoes. They showed the same picture on the morning news the next day. But my dulled senses were jarred by the terrified response of my then three-year-old daughter, who had come into the room without my noticing. She cried out, "Mommy, why are they doing that? Why are they so mad? Why are they being so naughty? Where is their mother?" And she ran and turned off the television in distress.

There was no mistaking my daughter's reaction—fear and terror. Suddenly I was reminded of the truth she saw so vividly. This is a scary world when people like us live in it. It just took the fresh eyes and perspective of someone new to the human scene to make me see it.

She also voiced a deep-seated question in the human psyche: isn't there any authority figure out there who will keep us safe and protect us from ourselves and one another? I may slip back into my complacency; sadly, it's all I've ever known. But my daughter asked what every religion and every great thinker has attempted to understand: how do we explain evil?

The only human record we have is marred from start to finish with evil. It's a study of people being aggressive, cruel, exploitive and lustful, seeking war instead of peace, vengeance rather than grace. Joseph Cooke, a Christian author and teacher, summarizes group evil astutely:

> I have never heard of any large group of people who, without external pressure or necessity, willingly agreed together to suffer major inconvenience or loss for the benefit of other groups who were worse off. . . . When the chips are down expediency always wins out over morality. . . . People in the mass look out for their own interest in the most shameless fashion. The only thing that ever stops them is power.[1]

And though there are magnificent exceptions, it is not radically different on the individual level. Why? Because, writes Ernest Becker, "if we care about anyone it is usually ourselves. . . . 2,500 years of history have not changed man's basic narcissism. . . . It is one of the meaner aspects of narcissism that we feel that practically everyone is expendable except ourselves."[2]

So it is not surprising that for all our knowledge and ideals, our record is one of murder and theft, blind destruction and betrayed ideals. We see there is a gap between what we espouse and how we live, between ideals and conduct, knowledge and behavior, intellect and character. "You can be smart but not be good," wrote William Carlos Williams. "It's something to have knowledge—another to be a good decent person," said Tolstoy.

Harvard psychiatrist Robert Coles agrees:

> I have seen plenty of arrogance and selfishness in the supposedly gentler, more "humanistic" professions—snobbishness or self-importance and meanness or hardness of spirit in doctors, in the clergy, in educators, in the so-called arts, and certainly, among us in my own branch of medicine, the psychoanalytic psychiatry. Years of personal analysis, of education, of postgraduate supervision have not prevented many of us from becoming dogmatic, smug and fiercely antagonistic to those who happen to disagree with us.

I try to keep such thoughts in mind when I ask future corporate leaders or financiers to take a sharp and candid look, or a smiling and wry one, at certain moral pitfalls. The labor leader, the political reformer, the egalitarian theorist, the medical healer, the minister or priest, the college teacher, even the moral philosopher or wise novelist are in the end all flawed human beings, no less in jeopardy as they go about their lives than those out there in the marketplace.[3]

Intimations of Immortality

Where does this bring us? For all the inadequacy of our idols and the darkness of our darker side, there still remain clues that tell us something about who we are. These clues are not sufficient to explain human evil, nor are they meant to be definitive, but I believe they inform us about another dimension of our nature.

Several examples of such clues, or signals, come to mind, ones that range across our human journey. I recall the time that my son, David, then almost two years old, looked up at a magnificent starry night at Tucker Farm. We had taken sleeping bags and spread them on the hillside on a midnight-black evening with not one electrical light in sight. He had been chattering away and suddenly rolled over on his back, gazed up and cried out, "Ohhh, Mommy!"

What enables one so young to recognize beauty and experience awe? One could say that it is merely the human response to aesthetics—but does that adequately explain the response of awe? Can everything that deeply moves us, that causes us to exult, be explained by social conditioning, genetics or biological impulses? Do we not sense that there is more to us than that?

Why is it that in crisis our first human instinct frequently is to pray? Or we call people who will pray for us because we feel they may have "closer connections" than we do! Why is it that the greatest moments of our lives—such as the birth of a child—and the worst moments of suffering so frequently draw us toward spiritual realities?

I have a friend who I think would describe herself as an agnostic. In the space of only three years she saw at least five dear friends and relatives die.

After she attended the last funeral she told me, "Do you know what I felt as I saw the coffin being lowered? Rage! It can't be meant to be like this. How can this person I love be snuffed out and gone? It isn't right. How can someone who was as alive and vital as my aunt simply be no more? How is it possible that we can never again enjoy each other's company? *It is wrong and I hate it!*"

She was voicing what lies in the heart of us all. Deep within, we know that there is something alien and abnormal about death. Why do we feel that way? How can something so commonplace be such an affront? We may not know exactly how things were meant to be, but with Dylan Thomas we "rage against the dying of the light."

What do these clues suggest? What are we to make of these responses to birth and death, to the moments when we experience mystery and awe or horror and loss? There seems to be something in our nature that registers these experiences more profoundly than we can say. Could it be that part of the problem for us moderns is that we lack words to put around the realities that move us the most? We talk about self, not soul; neurosis, not sin; life as biological drives, not spiritual realities. We have eliminated God and the spiritual realm, yet somehow we do not know what to do with all that our heart tells us is there. As Flannery O'Connor writes, "Mystery is a great embarrassment to the modern mind."[4] Becker concurs: "Modern[s] try to replace vital awe and wonder with a 'How to do it' manual."

Perhaps that is why we have reached for so many earthly solutions and rewards and found they do not satisfy. Most of our human happiness still leaves us aware that we are not fulfilled; we yearn for something more, we sense that something more was promised. But even beyond that, "our highest joys almost insist on eternity, for we touch such a point of ecstasy that time's boundaries of change and decay just *cannot be all,*" the English author and thinker Os Guinness said in a lecture.

If the world's near-best does not satisfy—whether through romance, sexuality, therapy, work or wealth—and our very best seems to reach beyond the world, then is it possible that we are more than material beings? Is it possible that we are not only biologically, philosophically, socially, physically real but also spiritually real?

What would this mean for our journey—investigating what is wrong with us? We can list our symptoms, but what is the nature of the illness? We have spent a fair amount of time looking at some of the modern explanations of why we are in trouble. In particular, we have invited Camus in the literary world and Becker in the psychological world to point out aspects of what is wrong with us. Yet while their insights are helpful and penetrating, we are left feeling that something deeper than analysis is required.

Reaching for the SOAP

Does evil come from outside or inside? Is it part of our essential human nature, or is it an alien intrusion? When we try to figure it out by ourselves, the answer eludes us. As Pascal says, "We remain incomprehensible to ourselves."[5] Yet living as we do in an age that is endlessly fascinated with self, one would think we could at least get close to the source of our problem. We have been told that all our woes are rooted in the biological, in the economic, in being neurotically driven, in genetic impurity, in a will to power. These interpretations offer insights into what it means to be human, yet none has proven sufficient.

What do we do when we have a medical problem? We go to a trustworthy outside authority for a diagnosis. We go to a doctor and describe our symptoms. What, in turn, does the doctor do? A physician once told me that the most helpful thing she learned in medical school was a form of diagnosis summed up by the acronym SOAP. She first listens to the S—the subjective data. So far our journey has led us to examine an array of subjective experiences: our discontent, our general feelings of malaise and anxiety. Next the doctor takes into account the O—the objective data that verify the patient's subjective discomfort. Medically, that would come through taking their vital signs, doing blood work and so on. Again, we have examined plenty of concrete data on the human condition to support our subjective experience: maladjusted behavior, neurosis, self-centeredness, tension and disharmony in relationships. A, my friend continued, stands for the assessment, a diagnosis based on the objective and subjective data that involves identifying the disease. Then comes P—the plan the patient will have to follow if he or she is to get well.

Are we ready to reach for the SOAP for our predicament? We have spent enough time on the *S* and the *O* to be able to say that we know our symptoms. What we need now is a diagnosis and then a plan for treatment. But as in the case of a physical illness, it is nearly impossible to make an accurate self-diagnosis; we need an outside source to help us. We are entrenched in our ruts; our vision is so limited and defined by our social background, culture and genes that unless we can obtain an outside diagnosis and treatment we will remain forever stuck with our symptoms without hope of understanding them.

It is now time to shift to that outside diagnostic perspective on ourselves. I want to turn to the Bible's diagnosis of the human condition, and I do so for several reasons. First, because what I am writing follows the story of my own journey, and this is exactly where my own journey brought me. Although I began my search by examining Eastern religions, I eventually made my way to the Bible partly because it was the only description of human personality that fit reality—able to unlock the mystery of both the Nazi-doctor side and the image-of-God side. And since it is what I know the best, it is what I believe I am most qualified to share.

There is another reason. The great surprise that came to me as an agnostic who had never read the Bible was how a document so ancient could be so modern. We have spent four chapters considering some of the devious means we employ to avoid admitting we have a problem. But the Bible *begins* by stating bluntly that we have a problem. And it quickly tells us what the source of our problem is. That in itself is intriguing. And since throughout Western civilization the Bible has been regarded as the single most extraordinary piece of literature ever written, why *shouldn't* we examine the Bible's diagnosis of the human condition?

A Name for It

The Bible tells us that we *can* know what our problem is, but not by stopping with the symptoms alone. If we do that we are left merely to peel away the infinite layers of an onion skin, or to travel endlessly down tortuous labyrinths of background and motive. These approaches, as we have seen, can lead to extremely valuable insights, but not to ultimate exits. The Bible begins the diagnosis by telling us what the healthy organism looks like. It shows us what we were created to be, what happened to change us and what the consequences have been. To understand what it says, we will take a look at the familiar story of creation (which shows us who we were intended to be) and the story of the fall (which shows us who we have become). Together, these stories give us the right framework and the right categories for understanding what it means to be human, including what is normal and what is abnormal, what is our real happiness, what is the cause of our problems. As Pascal said, "Certainly nothing offends us more rudely than this doctrine [original sin], yet without this mystery, the most incomprehensible of all, we are incomprehensible to ourselves."

What did God intend when he created the human race? According to the story of Adam and Eve, human beings were created by a good God and made in his image and likeness. Thus we were given the freedom to love, to reason, to create, to be unique and diverse yet crowned with moral perfection and so to live in harmony with God and the rest of his creation. Here creature and Creator knew real bliss. Our nature was good, although different from that of our Creator. Being made finite, dependent and not self-sufficient, we were to be fulfilled in God. Being made in his image, we are made to love and be loved, to trust and know protection, to know and be known, to live in joy and experience delight. God made us with these desires, and he intended to fulfill them. Thus the path to freedom and fulfillment comes when we live as we were created to be: in harmony with the center of all life—God—not simply centered on ourselves.

The story of Adam and Eve reveals not only the marvel of creation but also what went wrong. This is precisely what we have been looking for. The Bible tells us that at some point humans revolted by asserting their will over their Creator's. In defiance and arrogance (and stupidity) they tried to be equal with God. They wanted to call the shots. The heart of their sin lay in their claim to autonomy; in refusing to accept their creaturely condition before God. They refused to trust themselves to God's love. In not making God their center, they disobeyed him and contradicted the laws of their own nature.

Hold on, we protest. Surely you don't expect a modern person to believe that human woes could be tied to something as archaic as the notion of sin? Few concepts have less cash value today than *sin*. In fact, since the time of the Enlightenment we have not even used the concept of sin as a category for understanding the human condition. So let's not be so naive as to say our problems are a result of sin. Nobody believes *that* anymore.

Yet the notion of human fallenness has captured the imagination of literary thinkers such as Camus and William Golding, author of *Lord of the Flies*. It was exactly Karl Menninger's point in *Whatever Happened to Sin?* And listen to what psychotherapist Otto Rank says in Becker's *The Denial of Death:* "The neurotic type suffers from a consciousness of sin just as much as did his religious ancestor, without believing in the conception of sin. This is precisely what makes him 'neurotic'; he feels a sinner without the religious belief in sin for which he therefore needs a new rational explanation." Thus the plight of the modern person is that he or she is, according to Becker, "a sinner with no word for it." Becker even lists the characteristics of the disease as being in disharmony with others, always trying to create one's own world from within themselves, blowing oneself up to larger than true size, refusing to admit one's cosmic dependence.

So perhaps we are not dealing with something so ridiculous and outdated. Perhaps the Bible's candor has done us a service by not only addressing the problem but giving us a name for it.

Where It All Began

The Bible traces the problem back to Genesis 3 and the serpent's artful query: "Did God really say, 'You must not eat from any tree in the garden'?" That simple-sounding question masks a malevolent brilliance. By beginning so innocently, the devil plants the suggestion in Adam's and Eve's minds that surely God would not say this, not the God who loves them, who is for them. Through this tiny insinuation the serpent undermines their belief that God can be trusted to have their best interests at heart. And he incites them as creatures to query their Creator and make God's word subject to their judgment.

Then the serpent deliberately misrepresents God's strictness. God had never said Eve and Adam should not touch any tree, merely that they should not eat from the tree of life. But the serpent knows his strategy is proving effective when Eve says, "But God did say, 'You must not eat fruit from the tree that is in the middle of the garden, and you must not touch it, or you will die'" (Genesis 3:3). Thus she too exaggerates God's strictness (she was not told not to touch it) and becomes the first legalist in history. She has fallen prey to the suggestion that God isn't for us, so the serpent goes further and engages in outright contradiction of God. "You will not surely die. . . . For God knows that when you eat of it your eyes will be opened, and you will be like God, knowing good and evil" (Genesis 3:4-5).

That is now a direct attack on God's command and his motives. God is no friend, the devil suggests. He is jealous and doesn't want competition. So in a few brief lines God has gone from friend to enemy, and the devil finishes with a flat contradiction to which he adds a promise: "You will be like God."

Thus everything becomes twisted, turned upside down. Divine love is presented as jealousy, fulfillment in service to God as servility, and even a loss of innocence as life. History's first misinformation campaign has done its deadly work, and Adam and Eve's dream of enlightenment ends in frantic, pathetic attempts to run to cover and hide.

An Alien Force

It is crystal clear that Adam and Eve succumbed to outside temptation. There is no way around that fact. Good and evil were both realities by the time humans arrived on the scene. But the fact that the temptation came from a creature (the serpent) created by God throws light on several things: God creates all things for a good purpose, but beings with the freedom to choose also have the freedom to rebel. And one has clearly so chosen and rebelled already.

Now the passage does not state directly who the serpent embodies, although elsewhere in the Bible it is made clear that the snake represents the devil. Nor does it suggest that there are two equal power centers. God is clearly superior to evil, but there can be no understanding of the human dilemma without the passage's recognition of the presence and reality of evil. The irony of the story is that Adam and Eve listen to an animal (to whom they as higher creatures are superior) as it instructs them about the nature of the Creator. What a topsy-turvy turn of events! As someone once told me, Eve's response to the serpent should have been: "Wait a minute. You look so familiar. Don't I know you from somewhere? Oh yes, I remember now—didn't my husband name you yesterday?"

How do Adam and Eve react once their guilt is discovered? Not too well. Adam sets the human race off on its grand process of denial by pathetically attempting to deny there is a problem at all—and hiding from God. It is almost as if he thinks that if he can escape getting caught, maybe it did not really happen. Once he is discovered, his next line of defense is blame: "That woman—she gave it to me." And then he adds a final touch: "The woman *you* gave me, Lord" (see Genesis 3:12). From denial through blame to rationalization, his argument runs like this: If God cannot pick me a better partner, how can it be my fault? And his reactions are so smooth and deftly developed that one would never guess he is a rookie at the business of sin.

The story of Adam and Eve was written thousands of years ago, long before our therapeutic age. Yet it describes their reactions toward their rebellion in terms of what we now know as classic character defenses (the very responses we examined earlier as denial, scapegoating and so on). But the Bible makes it clear that these are merely guilt-laden reactions to the problem. They are not the core of the problem itself.

A Sorry Train of Consequences

What was the result of the decision to strike out and seek independence? Nothing remained the same. From that point on, all human relationships became distorted—relationships with God, with nature, with one another and with themselves. Sin came in and touched their existence on every level. It is not only a matter of personal sin, such as pride, envy, greed and lust. Evil spread to every level of creation, from the micro to the macro: oppression, injustice and mistreatment of widows, orphans and immigrants—those sins that my daughter cried out against on television news.

Another result of sin's rupture from God was fear and anxiety, traits all conscious creatures share. Why are we anxious? Because sin means we need to be God but aren't.

As Ernest Becker says:

> We consult astrology charts like the Babylonians, try to make our children into our own image with a firm hand like the Romans. . . . And we wonder why, with all this power capital drawn from so many sources, we are deeply anxious about the meaning of our lives. The reason is plain enough: none of these, nor all of them taken together, represent an integrated world conception into which we fit ourselves with pure belief.

Jesus made the same point even more simply when he said to his disciples, "Who of you by worrying can add a single hour to his life?" (Matthew 6:27).

Thus the Bible calls our problem *sin* and locates it at the very center of human personality. In essence, sin is the deliberate claim to the right to ourselves and the equally deliberate refusal to worship God as God. The story of Adam and Eve is therefore our story too. We may not have chosen so consciously to rebel, but we are rebels nonetheless. We too have made self the center and source of life in the place of God. It is that same rebellion against God that causes us to use the psychological defenses that keep us from seeing the truth about ourselves. The problem with humanity, the Bible says bluntly, is not a metaphysical problem (in other words, a design problem in our very being, which could be blamed on our Creator). It is inescapably a moral problem, and it is our fault.

What this means is that life as we currently experience it is not the way it was created to be. We are living on a planet that is in a state of dysfunction. Suffering, sorrow, disease and death are all around us, but it wasn't meant to be so! Since evil is a moral and not a metaphysical problem, it is abnormal—not God's original intent. Death was not a part of God's plan when he created us. The abnormality of sin gives death a sting, which explains the outrage that my friend felt at her friends' funerals. She was right: There is something terribly wrong about the way things are. Sin has come into the picture. Human rebellion has altered the very structure of reality. But God is not responsible for the mess. In fact, as we shall see, it is his desire to deal with it once and for all.

Is Sin So Serious?

Perhaps to talk like this makes you wonder why God makes such a big deal about sin. After all, we can forgive our own children their excesses. We don't get hassled over everything they do. We manage to forgive and forget—so why can't God loosen up a bit? He sounds pretty uptight. Who wants to know somebody who can't relax and let bygones be bygones?

Just imagine for a moment that you are God. That shouldn't be too hard to pull off—we pretend it all the time. Imagine the picture you had in mind as you created planet earth. Your desire, I would bet, was that your human creatures should live in harmony with you and one another. But then imagine that the universe that was your creation chose not to go your way. We human beings decided, in other words, that we didn't want you to be the center of our existence. So you've been compelled to watch for generation after generation, century after century, as people pollute and destroy nature, nations, one another and themselves.

You're now watching the entire globe at war. You see that we use the gifts you gave us—intelligence and imagination, tools that were created for good purpose—to destroy one another. You see human brilliance and skill used so fiendishly as to defy comprehension. You watch the Crusades carried out *in your name*, killing every living thing in sight. You see the Holocaust—human beings shoveling the children of other human beings into gas chambers, using babies for target practice. You see bright, alert young minds drugging themselves into oblivion. You watch us laboring earnestly to create tools that will obliterate the planet. But does your creation pause to think, let alone weep, kneel and ask forgiveness? On the contrary. We blame *you*.

No big deal, did someone say? The wonder is not that God takes sin so seriously but that he takes us even more seriously—so much that he was willing to pay the ultimate price to have sin dealt with. But that's to run ahead.

Warning: Contagious and Deadly

OK, our skeptic friend says, I get the point. It is clear this planet has gotten itself in a mess. And it may be true that the core of the problem is that we chose to put ourselves, not God, at the center. But couldn't I try to be a good person without making God the center of my life, at least until I get older? I have this awful dread that all the things I most love the Bible is going to label sin. Can't I enjoy life now until I am too tired to enjoy my minor peccadilloes? Then, as I approach death, I'll check in with God. I would get the best of both worlds. After all, your own Augustine said, "Give me chastity, Lord, but not yet."

Few people, of course, are quite that candid in words. But many people say it in roundabout ways, and many more do it without saying it. There are several deceptions going on here at once. To try to uncover them, we need to take a look at a hidden life dynamic.

All life is in constant movement, constant growth. Death is static; life never is. There is a restless, creative, growing dynamic to everything. Astronomers tell us that nothing remains the same; even the North Star is moving. Our own galaxy is itself revolving and makes one revolution in about 200 million years; our planet makes its annual rotation around the sun in one brief year. Change is the very essence of life.

We too are in constant motion, as anyone can see just by looking at the various life stages of the individual. We see it most dramatically in the first year of a child's life, but only a little less dramatically all the way through. A friend of mine once told me, "I've been married three times to the same man." It is easy to understand why she could think that. One day we feel we really understand each other; then a few weeks later we struggle in bewilderment and misunderstanding, only to break through again to a higher ground of understanding. Nothing can be put on hold and frozen. A symphony begins with one note but takes on a life of its own. A book begins with a word; a love affair with a first look. An entire life begins from a single seed.

Unfortunately, the same principle applies to evil. Six million Jews were exterminated by what began as a single idea in a man's head. From that seed evolved a grand project in which trains ran on time, ovens were built, jobs were filled, a continent nearly fell, all from one evil idea. Sissela Bok, in her brilliant book *Lying*, says that it is easy to tell one lie, but hard to tell only one. Once a choice has been made, it grows. The issue is never, What are the consequences next time? What if I violate my conscience just this once and do what I know is wrong? Those are impossibilities because of the dynamic reality of evil.

Camus understood the contagious element in evil. He understood that there are choices and consequences in every decision we make. In *The Plague* he likens evil to bacteria that are alive, spawning disease and always seeking to reproduce: "He knew . . . that the plague bacillus never dies or disappears for good: That it can lie dormant for years and years in furniture and linen chests, that it bides its time in bedrooms, cellar trunks, and book shelves . . . and it would rouse up its rats again and send them forth to die in a happy city."[6]

Camus's picture of human suffering caused by a deadly plague is remarkably close to the biblical doctrine of sin. Sin is like a cancer. Cancer cells don't lie dormant. If anyone lets the cancer go, the results will be deadly. Only if the disease is cut out or blasted out will it stop growing. If you were told your child had cancer and needed to be operated on, would your response be "Whatever you do, don't use the knife. Just wait a little while and it will probably go away"? How ludicrous. You would rush your child to the hospital and plead with the surgeon to spare nothing to save her life.

People make a fatal mistake when they assume sin is a flat and static reality. Deadly, virile, contagious, it is a power capable of altering the very structures of reality. What does the Bible say that sinful choices do to us? To an age trained to think of "sins" as moral peccadilloes, this dimension of sin will seem all but incomprehensible; but we are told that sin blinds us, warps our judgment, separates us from the presence of God. Death, of course, is the result of sin; and Adam's rebellion is said to affect even the productivity of the soil (Genesis 3:17-19).

Why So Hard to Detect?

But wait a minute. If sin is so deadly, why isn't it easier to detect? Surely any sane person who recognizes a cancerous growth on his or her body would rush to a doctor and demand surgery. If sin really is the source of our problem, why are we able to live with it so easily? And even if we are able to recognize it, why do we find it so appealing?

The Bible's answer is simple: sin has blinded and deceived us. Many thinkers have recognized this human bent toward self-deception. Historian Barbara Tuchman, for example, has observed that we are even deceived about what is best for us, which shows how ruthless sin's intent is; its aim is to destroy us.[7] But she and others cannot explain why we are deceived. The Bible does. It makes it clear that our self-deception is a byproduct of our revolt against God. We are not only enslaved by sin, we are even unaware that it is our condition.

Self-deception occurs in two places. First, it affects us inside. The very "mission control" of our self has been infiltrated and fundamentally disordered. All our early warnings and security systems against sin have been knocked out, so sin is able to enter undetected and move around quite unchallenged.

In this disordered state we operate on a me-for-me attitude that can justify and excuse anything if it's for our own gain. Remarkably, we are even able to regard ourselves as still innocent. I remember speaking to a friend at an airport. After twenty-five years of faithful marriage, he was having an affair. He regretted it, but he explained: "It just happened. We didn't plan it or pursue it; it simply happened."

I said to him, "I know just what you mean. One day you were talking to her and suddenly all your clothes fell off. The next thing you knew, as you turned around, a bed just appeared in a room."

The man laughed uneasily and said, "OK, you got me. I guess I had to have been making choices, whether I consciously realized it or not."

This man is a dear friend, and I could speak so directly because he knew how much I cared for him. But what does that kind of *reasoning* tell us about ourselves? Who do we think we're kidding when we say, in effect, "Well, there I was, just standing around being an innocent bystander when all of a sudden 'life' came and did this to me"?

Isn't that the same kind of "innocent guilt" we saw in the Nazi doctors who rationalized the Holocaust? "It just happened," we say. "Life overwhelmed me and I found myself its victim."

The probable counter to this charge is that if sin blinds us, how can we be held responsible? But why is it that such reasoning occurs only when the subject in question is ourselves? Let the fault be in someone else and everything changes. Suddenly we see it all very clearly.

King David is an excellent example. He had committed adultery, murder and treachery, so when the prophet Nathan came to confront him one would think he would only have to say, "David, you've really blown it!"

Yet Nathan takes a very different approach. He appeals to David as lawmaker and tells him a story about *someone else* who has sinned and taken what did not belong to him. Nathan takes on the role of the subversive because David had become deeply entrenched in his own self-deception and excuses. But let David hear of someone else doing exactly what he had done, and he was incensed! Outraged!

Which just shows us that we are not so blind that we cannot see, with seeming 20/20 vision, someone else's sin. And this then becomes a sobering reason why we are held responsible for our own condition. We may be deceived, but we are never *that* deceived. Even in our worst self-deception there is an intentional element.

As the example of David reminds us, believers are not exempt. An agnostic friend of mine told me, "I have a born-again friend, and every time he says, 'I prayed about it and the Lord really gave me peace,' I start to panic. Because it always means that he wins and I lose! Isn't it interesting that the Lord always seems to guide him in the path that serves him and not me?" As Ruth Burrows points out, "Over and over we must realize that in what we think of as love and service for God lurks a ravenous self, which would use God to inflate self."[8]

The Devil's "Sting"

There is a second place where sin tricks us. Presenting itself to us on the outside as a legitimate operation, it deceives us and we don't see it is a gigantic trap, the devil's "sting." It presents evil as good, lies as truth. It tells us that there is no harm and extraordinary profit in what it suggests. Sin may be destructive in its true nature, ugly and devastating in its consequences; but it passes itself off as fun, pleasurable, exciting, mature—anything but what it is.

What is fascinating is that this deception sometimes operates in the physical realm in a terrible parallel with the moral realm. The biomedical dynamics of the AIDS virus, for example, are chilling: First the deadly cell invades the body. But it does not announce itself as an enemy right away. It does not reveal its intention to attack and destroy the healthy cells. Rather, it presents itself deceptively by *imitating* the healthy cell, until the healthy cell is seduced into thinking of the destroyer as friendly. But once the healthy cell takes it in, the invading cell immediately infects it and hijacks all the cell's machinery and turns it into a virus factory dedicated to turning out copies of the infecting virus. In short, it actually takes the cell over and makes it another destroyer. What isn't immediately apparent is that the human system has been disabled. The descent toward death is progressive, but death is the final result. One shudders to think how closely this process follows the story of temptation and sin in Genesis 3.

That is the point, however, where the medical model breaks down. If we discover we have cancer, we do not blame ourselves. Nor do we ask the surgeon to forgive us before he operates. We have a physical disease with physical symptoms, and what we need is a straightforward physical treatment. There is no moral issue involved.

But in the case of sin we have a spiritual illness. It will not do simply to say, "Lose five pounds; start to jog; try God," as we might try the Mayo Clinic. The Bible's blunt diagnosis is that we are in revolt. Or as C. S. Lewis puts it, it is not just a self-improvement program we need; we are rebels who must lay down our arms. Our disobedience has infected the entire planet.

In short, we have reached the point where it is ridiculous to claim, as did the Frenchman whom Clamence mocked, "But you see, sir, my case is exceptional. I am innocent!"[9]

"All right," the skeptic responds, softening. "I do recognize that I keep trying to run the show. And although I would have never seen it on my own, if there is a God in the universe then I am a moral rebel. But I am tired of the confusion and hollowness, the lack of purpose. So what can I do? Just tell me what to do to remedy the situation, and I'll do it."

And there the Bible's response is startling again. Absolutely nothing!

But actually Clamence realized that too. He knew that his self-centeredness, his continual insistence on running the show, was far too deeply entrenched for him to be able to stop. He knew he couldn't defeat his self-absorption. Nor can we. We can't reach in and straighten a twisted nature. We simply lack the power. If we are to be restored to what we were intended to be, it will have to be done for us.

Now that throws "awareness" and "self-knowledge" into a very different light. What practical value do they have if we were happier suffering from our symptoms without all of the insight? At least we once lived in the daze of false hope. But now we are told we are responsible for a condition that we are powerless to change.

Curiously, the problem of addiction again sheds light on this complex paradox of responsibility and powerlessness, especially as it relates to change. Why? Because the path of recovery for all addicts lies in first admitting their powerlessness. They no longer deny that they have a problem. They know that help must come from the outside. Their only choice is whether they will seek that help from a source beyond themselves. They alone are responsible for that choice. No one else can make the decision for them.

Exactly the same is true of sin. We are responsible for our condition, but we are powerless to change it. Only help from outside ourselves can change us—the help of God. But it is up to us whether we seek such a solution. So long as we still hold out, thinking that our happiness rests in someone else's changing (maybe we are waiting for an emotionally distant parent to transform magically) or for some circumstance to alter, we will never get well. So long as we entertain any notion that our problems will be solved by someone else's doing what we think they should, we doom ourselves to despair.

Here is where we part company decisively with our contemporary culture. It tells us to ignore our self-doubts and to feel only positive thoughts about ourselves. I am saying the opposite. *Pay attention* to those lurking doubts. Listen closely to that nagging discontent. Yes, it is important to have healthy self-esteem. But the irony is that the best road to health lies in the direction of realism about the sickness. Those who want the last in their lives to be the best must face the worst first. It is only in giving up on ourselves that we can go beyond ourselves and find ourselves. But there is a special reason for such ironies—the ultimate irony of all, the cross. To that we turn next.

6

The Cross

The cross is the point where God and sinful man merge
with a crash and the way to life is opened—
but the crash is on the heart of God.
OSWALD CHAMBERS

We began our search wondering why our simple desire for love and happiness is so easily frustrated. We examined what prevents us from reaching what we long for. We saw that even by listing our symptoms we could not diagnose our own condition without outside help. So we went to the Bible for explanation of our plight. We learned that our illness is spiritual in nature and deadly. We are in a state of rebellion against God and actually pretend we are our own god. Whether or not sin breaks out in blatant wrongdoing, it is surely seen in our claim to the right to ourselves, in the endless ways we attempt to play God and put ourselves in the center instead of recognizing that our greatest need is to know God and put him at the center.

And as with a physical problem, we saw that we cannot change our condition apart from treatment. No superficial remedy will do. We cannot overcome our addiction to ourselves by sheer willpower. That only makes

it worse. Nor can we stop ourselves from being self-centered. Only a power
that is stronger than ourselves can help us overcome ourselves.

So the next question is, Where do we look for such a power? Is there a
plan for treatment? Here is where the words of Jesus begin to make sense.
Jesus called his message "good news" because help is at hand. He knew that
the fatal disease within human nature can be cured only by the Divine Surgeon. Our only hope of remedy is if God does something. And according to
Jesus, he has.

But what has God done? Both the remedy and the proof of his love
behind it are seen most compellingly in the cross—the death of Jesus. Yes,
at the point where criminal disgrace, excruciating pain and the sin of the
world pierced the heart of God's Son. That will seem an utter mystery, yet it
is the crux of the Christian faith. It did not make sense to the disciples ini-
tially, and it doesn't readily make sense to us. How can killing someone
make sick people well or sinful people forgiven? That sounds like mumbo-
jumbo. Yet the message is unmistakable: Only in the cross, however hidden, is there any means of deliverance, of wholeness and of peace. Only in
what looks like a dead end do we have the hope of a new start.

Not Quite as Easy as We Think

It's a funny thing how quickly we slide from resisting any help to presum-
ing that help is easy. Because of our basic narcissism, we assume God has
no problem forgiving us. It doesn't even cross our mind that this might
pose a problem for God. In fact, we have a remarkably cavalier approach to
God. Sometimes we expect God to hop to; we secretly feel he is lucky even
to have us consider him.

An aspect of this attitude is very much like the sentiment expressed by
the character Baby in F. Scott Fitzgerald's *Tender Is the Night*. Baby watches
her brother-in-law Dick sacrifice his whole life, his medical career, even his
emotional well-being to help her psychologically troubled sister Nicole.
And after Nicole has drained everything from him, she divorces him and
moves on to a new man. For a brief moment, however, Nicole feels a flicker
of remorse as she thinks about how much she took from Dick. Until Baby
says blithely: "That's what he was educated for."[1]

We are like that. *Of course* God forgives, we think—after all, that's his job, isn't it? Or as Voltaire cynically said, "C'est son metier" (it's his business).

Part of our insensitivity comes from our immense hubris: Another part comes from the fact that we have been in hiding from ourselves for so long that we do not see how desperate our situation is. We want God but without the hassle of looking at the mess. Yet another part comes from the fact that we have never encountered pure goodness before. To meet it is anything but comforting. It terrifies. To anyone who cannot bear his scrutiny, God as moral goodness would be a "supreme terror," as C. S. Lewis put it in *Mere Christianity*. Which leads us to ask the ethical question Clamence pondered: how can someone who is truly good forgive what is truly bad without morally compromising himself?

Everyone reflecting on a divine solution to the human predicament should wrestle with that question. Even the complex and difficult theories of what theologians call "the atonement" (how God changes the heart of an estranged humanity and enables us to be reconciled and "at one" with him) are simply attempts to explain the ultimate mystery of a dilemma: How can God reconcile the opposing demands of his justice, which must judge evil, and his love, which wants to save the evildoer? How can God forgive without compromising his holiness and yet judge evil without frustrating his love? How can he forgive wrong without moral compromise and yet love without being angry over what destroys us?

What Sort of a God Gets Angry?

That raises another problem. We tend to be taken aback by the thought that God could be angry. How can a deity who is perfect and loving ever be angry? Just look at us—we manage to be very understanding and accepting of our flaws. We take pride in our tolerance of the excesses of others. So what is God's problem?

Of course the Bible never suggests that God's anger is lightly provoked. Or that God is ready to pounce at the first misstep. On the contrary, we are told he is "slow to anger" (Exodus 34:6). And his anger does not come from having a bad temper. Indeed, God's anger issues from the intensity and depth of his love for us, as well as the height of his moral perfection and his outrage against evil. God's anger is not the kind that comes from feeling slighted or ignored, as in "You've really hurt my feelings this time." God's anger is a just anger, arising from perfect motives.

Our problem in pondering anything about God is that we bring our human pettiness, jealousies and problems into the analysis. We can't help that, but it makes it difficult to imagine God having emotions similar to ours without the pollution ours bring. Even so, it may help to examine a comparable form of human anger. Think of how we feel when we see someone we love ravaged by unwise actions or relationships. Do we respond with benign tolerance as we might toward strangers? Far from it. We are dead against whatever is destroying the one we love.

Loving people who are drug addicts is a good example. It is one of the most frustrating, infuriating experiences I have ever known. I have seen two talented, bright people not be able to remember what we had been talking about a few hours before because of the effect of drugs. I have seen them so frantic to get to a bathroom to snort cocaine that they nearly knocked me over to get there. I have watched their noses dripping and listened to their self-inflated, drug-induced statements. And in their drugged deception, they were convinced they were acting normally. I don't think that to this day they are aware that I knew what was going on. If they were, they would say it was a gross exaggeration. They were in total control, they thought. Their use of drugs was just "recreational," they believed, though as a matter of fact it was the daily ritual of their addiction.

How did I feel? I was grieved and sickened to see the wasted potential. But I also felt fury. Everything in me wanted to shake them, to say, "Can't you see? Don't you know what you're doing to yourself? You become less and less yourself every time I see you." I wasn't angry because I hated them. I was angry because I cared. If I hadn't loved them, I could have walked away. But love detests what destroys the beloved. Real love stands against the deception, the lie, the sin that destroys. Nearly a century ago the theologian E. H. Gifford wrote, "Human love here offers a true analogy; the more a father loves his son, the more he hates *in him* the drunkard, the liar, the traitor."[2]

The fact is that anger and love are inseparably bound in human experience. And if I, a flawed and sinful woman, can feel this much pain and anger over someone's condition, how much more a morally perfect God who made them? If God were not angry over how we are destroying ourselves, then he wouldn't be good and he certainly wouldn't be loving. Anger isn't the opposite of love. Hate is, and the final form of hate is indifference.

Clamence contemplated this dilemma of forgiveness but stuck rigidly to his own perspective on it. He was concerned that divine forgiveness of his sins would be accomplished by an airy wave of a celestial wand and suddenly everything wrong would be made right. Thus, as the object of divine forgiveness, he would become the victim of a celestial snow job. That offended his sense of justice. And if it were so, it would offend ours too.

But we need to switch viewpoints and ask what forgiving us does to God. How can a good God forgive bad people without compromising himself? Does he just play fast and loose with the facts? "Oh, never mind," he might say. "Boys will be boys." Try telling that to a survivor of ethnic cleansing in the former Yugoslavia or to someone who lost an entire family in Rwanda.

No. To be truly good one has to be outraged by evil and utterly and implacably hostile to injustice. People can't call themselves good and have an iota of indifference to evil of any sort. And that is precisely what the Bible tells us about God—so we are back to our problem (Ezekiel 7:8-9).

When Justice and Mercy Clash

The truth is that in human terms there is no resolution to the tension between justice and mercy. In both life and literature the tension is common and insoluble. Victor Hugo's novel *Les Miserables* provides a poignant example that has been powerfully presented in the musical based on it. Long before the beginning of the story, Jean Valjean stole one loaf of bread for his sister and her seven starving children and was sent to prison. Because he tried several times to escape, his sentence was extended to nineteen years. Valjean has become embittered and hardened by his prison experience. Once out of prison, at his lowest moment, he steals silver cutlery from the only person who has ever been kind to him, a bishop, Monseigneur Bienvenu. He is promptly caught, but the bishop covers for him and says he is innocent. After his encounter with the bishop, Valjean decides to lead a new life. He adopts a new name, becomes mayor of a town and seeks to distance himself from his former life.

However, there was a police officer, Javert, at the scene when the police arrested Valjean for stealing the bishop's silver. Javert assumed correctly that Valjean was guilty, but he had no way of proving it. Years pass. One day Javert meets the distinguished mayor and begins to suspect that it is really the convict Jean Valjean. Through a remarkable turn of events Valjean's identity is exposed. But rather than go back to prison, which is what Javert intends, Valjean escapes. For the rest of the novel Javert pursues him, determined to find him and make him pay for his crime of thievery and false identity.

To understand Javert, one must see that he is single-mindedly committed to justice, out to punish any and every infraction of the law. His moral world is stark. It contains no ambiguity, no shading, no compromise and certainly no mercy. If a crime is committed, the culprit has to pay. Even though Jean Valjean has become an exemplary citizen, to forgive him is not in the realm of possibility for Javert. Jean Valjean has violated the law. Jean Valjean has to be punished. To forgive the criminal would wipe out the distinction between right and wrong. To forgive the criminal's debt would be to condone his evil and lead to a world of moral chaos. Evil must be seen for what it is, condemned and rooted out.

Fortunately, Javert's harshness does not represent the heart of God. Javert almost seems to delight in finding fault, accusing and judging. Nothing could be further from God than this lack of mercy. Nonetheless, Javert reminds us of an important biblical truth: evil is serious. Left unattended, evil destroys, and we cannot afford to be sentimental about it.

The bishop reflects the opposing pole of the tension: kindness and mercy. The bishop gave Valjean another chance. He did not condemn him or give him what he deserved; he was lavishly kind to him. He did not give Valjean another chance *after* he had changed his behavior. He showed mercy and let him go free even though there was sure proof that he was the thief. Valjean had treated the bishop abominably. He had showed the bishop nothing but contempt and ingratitude. The bishop had no reason to hope that Valjean might change his ways. He did not know that Valjean had originally been in prison only for a misdemeanor. As far as he knew, it could have been for murder. But the nature of the crime was irrelevant to the bishop. His mercy was not based on the scale of the crime or on the statistical probabilities that a man like Valjean might change. He was kind the first time, without knowing Valjean, and Valjean betrayed his trust. The second time the bishop knew whom he was dealing with. But he still chose to gamble further and raise the stakes with even more freedom and mercy.

Why was the bishop so kind and trusting the second time? Because he was trusting God, not Valjean. He knew God can change anyone if only the person will let him. He also knew that God's goodness and mercy are more powerful than sin, if only the person turns to God. The bishop believed that God's image in us is not effaced. There is always "a primitive spark, a divine element . . . which can be developed by goodness, kindled, lit up, and made to radiate, and which evil can never entirely extinguish."[3] He believed that God can transform human nature inside and out. Thus the bishop represents the grace of God, his undeserved favor given to undeserving people.

The same conflict between justice and mercy recurs again and again in real life. Once in a courtroom I heard a person being sentenced for a crime. In some ways it was like reliving the story line of *Les Miserables*. On the one hand, the viewpoint of absolute justice seemed to reign supreme. It was bone chilling to see the impersonal nature of the law. A crime had been committed, and the person had to pay. Justice did not care if the person being tried was someone's son or daughter, sibling or friend. It was irrelevant whether the person was deeply sorry and would clearly never do it again or if he was carrying emotional baggage of his own. He had violated the law. He had to pay.

But another principle and perspective was present in that courtroom. It was almost, but not quite lost. It was the law of love. Just as the judge was giving the sentence, a middle-aged man suddenly broke into racking sobs. He was clearly the father of the person on trial, and his anguish changed everything. For a split second we all saw the defendant through a different lens. This was not just a defendant who had committed a crime. This was somebody's child grown up, a child still adored and treasured by a father. Even the judge paused, but he had his job to do and he resumed sentencing. Later, as everyone filed out, I heard the father say, "I have never felt so helpless in my entire life. If only I could have done something. I would have gladly paid the price if I could."

Enter the bishop. That was the first time I had ever been in a courtroom. But the overwhelming memory that I carry with me was not the trial itself but the response of the parent wishing he could have taken the place of his child.

The Unresolvable and the Unthinkable

The trouble is, the judge and the father could no more be reconciled in their responses in life than Javert and Jean Valjean in the novel. The judge would argue like Javert: unless we clearly condemn evil and show that wrongdoing carries a terrible price, we relegate ourselves to a world of moral chaos. And they would be correct. But what about the father? How can a parent's love ever be silenced in the face of a harsh prison sentence? Many times I have heard older men say, "I really believe in playing hardball with criminal offenders. A little time in the slammer is what they need." Yet let the offender in question be such a man's child and the picture changes entirely—as it should. The judge and the father both have appropriate responses. The judge's job is to sentence. The parent's heart is to stand in for the child.

Stand in for the child? There is our clue. When love comes face to face with crisis and suffering in the one who is loved, its first impulse is to stand in, to substitute. Don't we sometimes wish we could bear the suffering of a loved one if it would spare them the trauma? I have never met a parent who did not say of their critically ill child, "How I wish it could have been me instead."

But that is exactly what God felt. *And that is exactly what God did.* He took our place. When the judgment had to fall, he became our substitute and it fell on him. Only the unthinkable can overcome the unresolvable, and we are left with the remarkable fact: We are the proud sinners, but the final victim of our sin and pride is God. A willing victim. The concept of substitution, or standing in, lies at the heart of the highest love of all and therefore at the heart of our salvation. As John Stott points out:

> For the essence of sin is man substituting himself for God, while the essence of salvation is God substituting himself for man. Man asserts himself against God and puts himself where only God deserves to be; God sacrifices himself for man and puts himself where only man deserves to be. Man claims prerogatives which belong to God alone; God accepts penalties which belong to man alone.[4]

Now we understand why we can be confident of God's love and forgiveness. For in looking at the cross we get our deepest glimpse into the character of God. How can we be sure that God's nature is loving? "Because the good news of the Gospel is that God takes our sinfulness into himself; and overcomes in his own heart what cannot be overcome in human life, since human life remains within the vicious circle of sinful self-glorification on every level of moral advance."[5] Because God takes evil seriously but us even more seriously. So that when he judges evil harshly, he sacrifices even his Son to do what it takes to free us. He did not soften his judgment and condemnation of sin. But he let the judgment fall on his Son. That's what substitution means.

Everything Is in the Who

To understand what the cross means and how it can "work," we must understand who took our place and why. And in particular, why no one else could have done it.

First, it was essential that the substitute be divine, partly because only someone who was free of sin himself could take on himself the sin of another, and partly because our problem is so deep that no human can solve it. We might speculate as to how nice it would have been of George Washington to want to stand in for our sins. If, say, he saw how desperate our human condition was and said, "Oh, please, let me take care of it. You have ignored God. But don't worry, I'll take the punishment you deserve," our response might be, "Gee, thanks, George, it's nice of you to want to do something." But for all our respect for the father of the American nation, wouldn't that offer be pretentious? How would his standing in for us solve anything if he has the same problem we do? For a fellow mortal to make such an offer would be both pretentious and forlorn. Our problem is so serious that it requires the help of someone with a perfect life to satisfy the justice of God.

Second, it was also essential for our sake that the substitute be human. We need someone completely identified with our condition, partly because one person has then gone through it without sin, and partly because we need someone so sympathetic that we can be sure he is on our side. The process cannot get off the ground unless we know we are loved and feel safe, not accused and condemned.

The best way for us to feel understood is to find someone who has been where we are, who knows what it is to be in our place. We appreciate empathy. We open up to compassion. It is a mystery why identification makes such a difference, but there is nothing quite like it. When a parent loses a child, everyone tries to offer words of support and sympathy. But about the only people able to enter into the pain are other parents who have lost a child. Similarly, who can understand the trials of being an alcoholic or living with one, or feeling caught in a prison of inexplicable rage or living with an abusive spouse, or having a fatal illness or living with someone who does, except the people who have been through it? The solution must involve someone who has been there.

As invaluable as empathy is, we need something else. Our road to recovery is profoundly enhanced when we meet people who not only have suffered but have emerged better people as a result. We need more than commiseration, we need someone to show us that our pain can be redeemed and there is light ahead of us. And the ones who show this best are those who have lived deeply and have not sidestepped suffering. Those who, once the going got tough, faced themselves and their trials fully, but in faith. My experience has been that these people radiate joy, serenity and wholeness. When they speak, I listen. They have both authority and sensitivity. The people who have helped me most in my own journey are those who tell me how God has made sense out of their suffering. They give me courage, not only because of what they have undergone but because of what they have overcome.

We can translate our human experience and apply it toward a divine solution only up to a certain point. For though there are people who can give us insight and inspiration, even the most compassionate of them are not powerful enough to change our insides and infuse us with the strength to live new lives. Only God can do that.

Only one person could fill the bill—and the miracle of the cross is that he did. "Been where we are"? He's literally taken our place. For the gospel reveals that our stand-in is fully God and fully man. He is fully human—sharing our life experience, our ordeals, our sorrow. He knows firsthand what it means to be human. When we read biblical accounts of the life of Jesus, we are surprised that he did not reveal his deity at the outset. Rather, Jesus progressively shows his deity as he enters into our situation, understanding our fears. "In a word we see him entered so deeply into our lot, that we are softened and drawn by him, and even begin to want him entered more deeply, that we may feel him more constrainingly. In this way a great point is turned in our recovery. Our heart is engaged before it is broken. We like the Friend before we love the Saviour."[6] He is the God-man.

Jesus was not human in the sense of being flawed. He shows us humanity as we were meant to be. He shows us what humanity looks like without sin, and it is breathtaking and marvelous.

That Jesus was without sin is logical if his nature was divine and crucial if he was to overcome evil. A sinful human could not satisfy the demands of divine justice. Jesus took the judgment of evil even though he was not evil and had never known sin. He bore the judgment we deserve in order to bring the forgiveness we do not deserve. God judges sin but reveals the depth of his love for us by bearing the judgment in our place: "While we were still sinners, Christ died for us" (Romans 5:8). Christ was fully God and fully human, yet without sin. That is why he is uniquely qualified to represent both God and humanity and to mediate between the two. He did not mediate in the sense that he tried to change God's mind about us, or that he kept arguing with God until he finally talked him into loving us. God's attitude toward us has always been love. It was not God's mind that needed to be changed but our hearts. As Stott points out, God did not start loving us after Jesus went to the cross. God's love for us sent him there: "The atonement did not procure grace, it flowed from grace." Unless we understand who Christ is, the cross will make no sense. The Bible says of Jesus, "For God was pleased to have all his fullness dwell in him" (Colossians 1:19). Yet he is fully human.

So what do we see as we look at the cross? The resolution of the dilemma of justice and mercy. The answer to both Javert and the bishop at once. The psalmist says it best: "Love and faithfulness meet together; righteousness and peace kiss each other" (Psalm 85:10). In the One who stands in for us we see a sacrifice that redeems us without compromising God's own character. According to Stott, "Divine love triumphed over divine wrath by divine self-sacrifice."

The Cross Makes Murderers of Us All

Several years ago after I had finished speaking at a conference, a lovely woman came to the platform. She obviously wanted to speak to me, and the moment I turned to her, tears welled up in her eyes. We made our way to a room where we could talk privately. It was clear that she was sensitive but tortured. She sobbed as she told me the following story.

Years before, she and her fiancé (to whom she was now married) had been youth workers at a large conservative church. They were a well-known couple and had an extraordinary impact on the young people. Everyone looked up to them and admired them tremendously. A few months before they were to be married, they began having sexual relations. That left them burdened enough with a sense of guilt and hypocrisy. But then she discovered she was pregnant. "You can't imagine what the implications would have been of admitting this to our church," she said. "To confess that we were preaching one thing and living another would have been intolerable. The congregation was so conservative and had never been touched by any scandal. We felt they wouldn't be able to handle knowing about our situation. Nor could we bear the humiliation.

"So we made the most excruciating decision I have ever made. I had an abortion.

"My wedding day was the worst day of my entire life. Everyone in the church was smiling at me, thinking me a bride beaming in innocence. But do you know what was going through my head as I walked down the aisle? All I could think was *You're a murderer. You were so proud that you couldn't bear the shame and humiliation of being exposed for what you are. But I know what you are and so does God. You have murdered an innocent baby.*"

Now she was sobbing so deeply that she could not speak. As I put my arms around her a thought came to me very strongly. But I was afraid to say it. I knew that if it was not from God it could be very destructive. So I prayed silently for the wisdom to help her.

She continued. "I just can't believe that I could do something so horrible. How could I have murdered an innocent life? How is it possible I could do such a thing? I love my husband; we have four beautiful children. I know the Bible says that God forgives all of our sins. But I can't forgive myself! I've confessed this sin a thousand times, and I still feel such shame and sorrow. The thought that haunts me the most is, *how* could I murder an innocent life?"

I took a deep breath and said what I had been thinking. "I don't know why you are so surprised. This isn't the first time your sin has led to death, it's the second." She looked at me in utter amazement. "My dear friend," I continued, "when you look at the cross, all of us show up as crucifiers. Religious or nonreligious, good or bad, aborters or nonaborters—all of us are responsible for the death of the only innocent who ever lived. Jesus died for all of our sins—past, present and future. Do you think there are any sins of yours that Jesus didn't have to die for? The very sin of pride that caused you to destroy your child is what killed Christ as well. It does not matter that you weren't there two thousand years ago. We all sent him there. Luther said that we carry his very nails in our pockets. So if you have done it before, then why couldn't you do it again?"

She stopped crying. She looked me straight in the eyes and said, "You're absolutely right. I have done something even worse than killing my baby. My sin is what drove Jesus to the cross. It doesn't matter that I wasn't there pounding in the nails, I'm still responsible for his death. Do you realize the significance of what you are telling me, Becky? I came to you saying I had done the worst thing imaginable. And you tell me I have done something even worse than that."

I grimaced because I knew this was true. (I am not sure that my approach would qualify as one of the great counseling techniques!) Then she said, "But Becky, if the cross shows me that I am far worse than I had ever imagined, it also shows me that my evil has been absorbed and forgiven. If the worst thing any human can do is to kill God's Son, and *that* can be forgiven, then how can anything else—even my abortion—not be forgiven?"

I will never forget the look in her eyes as she sat back in awe and quietly said, "Talk about amazing grace." This time she wept not out of sorrow but from relief and gratitude. I saw a woman literally transformed by a proper understanding of the cross.

What was it that changed in this woman? I believe her deepest pain, even more than over her guilt and the death of her child, came from her deception. There were two parts to her deception. Why was she so dismayed by what she had done? It arose from her thinking, *How could someone as nice and good as I do something so terrible?* So the first change came in her basic understanding of herself. The second deception had to do with the nature of evil itself. Evil is hard to see because in its early forms it seems so innocuous and mundane. Who would have guessed that concern over what others would think of her (pride) would have led to the death of an unborn baby?

Evil always takes us by surprise like that. It always seems so small and inconsequential at the moment of choice—later leaving us amazed by the enormous ramifications of our choices. That is why the cross brought such a relief to this woman. She saw its paradox: "that extraordinary love that insists on highlighting our evil, *in order* to leave us in no doubt that it has been forgiven."[7]

Accepted at Our Worst

Amazing as it sounds, we come with remorse and guilt over one thing and the Bible tells us we are far worse, much guiltier than we could have ever imagined. But surely this only confirms the accusation that the Christian faith is psychologically unhealthy. How are we ever to recover any healthy self-esteem with an attitude like that? What would ever possess a person to call a message like this "good news"?

The fact is that in the cross God demonstrates the deepest law of acceptance. For to be convinced that I have been accepted, I must be convinced that I have been accepted at my worst. This is the greatest gift an intimate relationship can offer—to know that we have been accepted and forgiven in the full knowledge of who we are, an even greater knowledge than we have about ourselves. This is what the cross offers.

I think the woman at the conference understood it intuitively and thereby walked into the heart and mystery of the cross. She thought that she was far too bad ever to be forgiven, that somehow her sin had taken even God by surprise. But the surprise was on her. For what God reveals through the cross is that we are far worse than we ever imagined and yet forgiveness is offered to us.

Did the revelation of her deeper guilt produce psychological unhealth in the woman? On the contrary, she experienced relief, joy and gratitude. She no longer felt condemned, she felt free! *Why?* Because there is nothing others can do to you when you have seen the worst about yourself and it has been forgiven. Sin always seeks to disguise itself, but nowhere is it more unmasked than at the cross.

We finally see the very being we dreaded to discover. At last we find out who we are. The cross brings us out of hiding. It breaks our denial, but only *in the very instant* that it shows us the possibility of forgiveness. It shows us our corruption, but in the same breath it tells us the price has been paid. We may keep on foolishly building a case for ourselves and pursuing our path of self-justification, but the cross will still be standing there waiting for us to come to the end of ourselves, kneel and repent. The Christian view of sin is radical but not pessimistic, because to see sin in Christian terms is to see that sin can be forgiven. That really is freedom. That really is amazing grace.

That means we can face our problems squarely. That means we can confess the darkest, most humiliating realities of our lives without despair and paralysis. No one can say, "All this talk about God being loving is very touching, but if he *really* knew me he would change his tune fast." The biblical message to us is, "I do know you. I know you far better than you know yourself. And you're in worse shape than you even realize. But do you think you have done something worse than killing my Son? And if I am willing to forgive you for that, then how can I not forgive you for anything else?" The words of the biblical prophet Micah show he must have experienced that: "Who is a God like you, who pardons sin?" (Micah 7:18).

We crucified Jesus and he died. And the good news is that because of the price God was willing to pay we can be forgiven and reconciled back to God. But to experience and benefit from the cure, we must turn to him and quit pretending there is nothing wrong with us. That is true sacrilege, pretending that there is nothing wrong with us when rectifying our problem cost God the life of his Son. God's mercy and justice are finally reconciled through the cross. Why did God take such dramatic effort to rescue us? Because he wanted so much to forgive us. And the amazing thing is, we did not even know we needed it.

Willful or Willing?

The next step on the road is obvious. What is our response to be to such extravagant forgiveness? Gerald May, in *Will and Spirit*, sets out the two main responses to life in the light of God's grace: willfulness or willingness.[8] If we believe that self is all there is, then the will becomes central and willfulness is the result. But when we realize that we are involved in something more than the ego, something better and beyond ourselves, that we can be in relationship to God himself, then the natural response is humility.

Hugo shows us both these responses in *Les Miserables*. The "willful response" can be seen when the gendarme Javert finally catches up with the criminal Valjean. Valjean has been hunted and pursued all his adult life by Javert, but suddenly he has the opportunity to kill his pursuer. To do so would mean the end of his torment; he could live as a free man, no longer fleeing Javert's relentless pursuit. But he chooses to spare Javert's life instead.

Valjean's kindness to Javert is an intolerable burden: Javert's benefactor is a convict! Javert's clear, rigid adherence to moral justice came crashing against a new vision: "returning good for evil, returning pardon for hatred, loving pity rather than vengeance, preferring to destroy himself rather than destroy his enemy." Valjean has opened up a new way of looking at life that terrifies Javert: "compassion . . . no more final condemnation, no more damnation, the possibility of a tear in the eye of the law, a mysterious justice according to God going counter to justice according to men."

Well, Javert will have none of it. Such an approach disgusts him. To forgive evil is to compromise morally. Grace is too soft, too weak. He wants justice. He doesn't want a compassionate convict doing him any favors. He pays his own debts. He doesn't want help from anyone. But now the intolerable, the unthinkable, has happened. He is indebted (for his very life!) to a convict. His world is turned upside down.

He will not accept mercy from a guilty man. So he takes the only choice he feels he has left: he kills himself. Why? Part of the reason is that he could not see any way to reconcile justice and mercy. But there is no doubt another reason too. To admit his need for mercy in relation to Valjean would be unthinkable, but to admit his need for mercy from God is equally intolerable. He would have to see *himself* as guilty. And that is out of the question.

So long as Javert could regard himself as pure and could see evil only as something "out there" to be condemned and exterminated, his system worked. He wanted to be the avenger who in righteous indignation could execute judgment and punishment. But for him to do so, it was imperative that he never see his own guilt, only the guilt of others. He was absolutely convinced that he was right. His world was made up of good and bad people. He was good; most of the rest were bad. He was clever; the rest were fools. And as far as he was concerned, people could not change. So when a bad person seemed to become good, and when this bad person showed him mercy, Javert's life fell apart. But the seed of his downfall was in his steely pride that steadfastly prevented him from admitting his own guilt and taking his place alongside the rest of the guilty human race. Thus his refusal to admit his sin made him harden. When he encounters mercy, he chooses willfulness. He must be in charge to the very end, responsible even for his own death.

The "willing response" can be seen at the pivotal moment in the novel, when Valjean meets the bishop after stealing the silver. By the time the bishop meets him, Valjean has become an embittered criminal. His version of justice is not that of Javert's self-righteous zealot. It is more along the lines of, why not rip off the bishop when everyone has ripped off me? So he steals the silver cutlery. But what happens when the police bring him to the bishop with the stolen goods? Everyone, Valjean most of all, is waiting for words of condemnation that will send him back to prison. To Valjean's astonishment the bishop tells the police that he gave the silver cutlery to Valjean as a gift and then adds, "Yes, but I gave you the candlesticks too . . . why didn't you take them along with your cutlery? Now go in peace. By the way, my friend, you needn't come through the garden. You can always come and go by the front door." And Valjean is freed.

Valjean deserves punishment, but he receives mercy. Ultimately it changes his life, for in the bishop's response he recognizes a celestial kindness. In Valjean's initial response to forgiveness, Hugo reveals what lies in every heart's response to grace: humiliation and pride. "He could not have said whether he was touched or humiliated." He does not understand why the bishop has treated him so kindly. He deserves punishment, to be sent back to prison where he belongs. Let him pay for his wrongdoing! Inwardly he stubbornly resists the gentle words and kind deeds.

> In opposition to this celestial tenderness he summoned up pride, the fortress of evil in man. He dimly felt the priest's pardon was the hardest assault, the most formidable attack he had ever sustained; that his hardness of heart would be complete if it resisted this kindness; that if he yielded he would have to renounce the hatred with which the acts of other men had for so many years filled his soul; and in which he found satisfaction; that this time, he must conquer or be conquered.

Hugo shows us with penetrating insight that we are moved by God's offer of forgiveness through the cross and we despise it at the same time. To accept forgiveness is the final blow to our pride. Forgiveness shows us that there is nothing we can do to earn God's acceptance. Forgiveness reveals not only our inability to change our nature but our inability to pay our debts. Valjean has done nothing to deserve those candlesticks. In fact he did the opposite. For the bishop to show kindness in light of his behavior seems a total folly. Which is why it hurts.

Most of us are like that. We do not want any favors. We want to do it ourselves. We want to pay our own debts. So our pride hates forgiveness. According to Stott, "We insist on paying for what we have done. We cannot stand the humiliation of acknowledging our bankruptcy and allowing someone else to pay for us. The notion that this somebody else should be God himself is just too much to take. We would rather perish than repent, rather lose ourselves than humble ourselves."

God's grace is devastating, for its undeserved kindness exposes our stiff-necked pride and pigheaded obstinacy. If only the bishop had made Valjean pay for his crime. If only he had required him to go to prison camp for fifty years to pay back the debt. It would have been a harsh sentence, but it might have been a secret relief, because it would have given Valjean the freedom to go on hating. And it would put him back in the position of control. It would be his work and no one else's to repay the debt.

The core of human religion has always been moralism and legalism. We like the "I must try harder" approach to religion because it is rooted in pride and control. It teaches that by self-effort alone we can make ourselves good. We favor this kind of religion because that way we do not really need God, we just need to live up to the standards we choose (which of course we cannot do either!).

But the bishop does not offer Valjean a life of religious duty that really would be a self-help cure in religious guise. Instead he calls him to admit his guilt, to give up his bitterness and stubborn pride, all that makes up the walls of his defenses. He is asked to give up control and surrender his life to God. And through the response of Valjean to God's offer of salvation, he can begin to live for good and not for evil.

Grace is devastating because it scales the walls of our highest defenses, but the power of its devastation is in the depths of its love. In grace we see the face of love and love alone. God does not want to give us what's coming to us. He wants to give us the silver candlesticks. His love is that lavish and extravagant. *Les Miserables* puts sin in its proper light. As low as Jean Valjean sinks, God's grace is mightier. Valjean's badness is simply no match for

God's goodness. Our evil is like a blip on the screen next to the endless panorama of the love of God. Hugo shows us that the greater mystery is never our evil but God's goodness.

Hugo is relentless in his conclusions. Our human will is of critical importance, and we have only two choices. We may choose to go the "willful" way with Javert: *No! I insist on paying my own way. No matter how great my debt or how impossible it is to pay, I will not accept favors from anyone, not even from God. I will not surrender, I must be in control!* But that way ends in certain suicide. Or at least in an inner death in the midst of life.

Alternatively, we may enter with Valjean into the "willing" way of life: *Yes, I admit my guilt. And I accept God's amazing grace that I do not deserve and never could have earned. And I surrender my life to God through Christ for him to do with as he pleases.* That way leads to life. But the choice is ours. No one can make it for us.

As for Valjean, he chooses life.

> Jean Valjean's heart swelled and he burst into tears. It was the first time he had wept in nineteen years. . . . He wept for a long time. He shed hot tears, he wept bitterly, more terrified than a child. . . . His past life, his first offense . . . his exterior degradation, his interior hardening, his release made sweet by so many schemes of vengeance . . . all this returned and appeared to him, clearly, but in a light he had never seen before. He could see his life, and it seemed horrible; his soul, and it seemed frightful. There was, however, a gentler light shining on that life and soul. It seemed to him that he was looking at Satan by the light of Paradise. . . . One thing was certain . . . that he was no longer the same man, that all was changed in him.
>
> How long did he weep? What did he do after weeping? Where did he go? Nobody ever knew. It was simply established that, that very night, the stage driver who at that hour rode the Grenoble route and arrived at Digne about three in the morning, on his way through the bishop's street saw a man kneeling in prayer, on the pavement in the dark, before the door of Monseigneur Bienvenu.

Valjean would know further pain and suffering throughout his life, but from that moment on he faced it as a changed man. And when he drew his last breath, the light that fell across his face was the glow from the silver candlesticks. He died, but grace had won.

7

The Resurrection

There are no ordinary people. You have never talked
to a mere mortal. It is immortals whom we joke with,
work with, marry, snub, and exploit—
immortal horrors or everlasting splendors.
C. S. Lewis

One of the courses I audited at Harvard was called "Systems of Counseling." We were looking at a case study in which the therapist, using an approach called psychodynamic psychotherapy, helped the patient uncover a hidden hostility toward his mother. Naming the problem and understanding the mechanisms of what really bothered him seemed to make the patient feel as if a great weight had been lifted.

Then the professor began to proceed to the next case. Mustering my courage, I raised my hand and said, "I don't quite know how to phrase this in the appropriate psychobabble, but let's say the patient returned a few weeks later and said, 'I'm so relieved to understand what was bothering me. My mother did things that provoked my hostility. But now I'd like to get beyond my anger. I'd like to be able to love her and forgive her. How do I do that?' How does psychodynamic psychotherapy help a person with a request like this?"

There was silence. Then the professor answered, "I think the therapist would say, 'Lots of luck!' It's accomplishing a great deal in life just to be able to get past our defenses to uncover and name the hidden things that drive us, to identify our anxieties, fears and problems at the root level and not the symptom level. So to ask that his hostility magically disappear isn't realistic. He'll have to learn to live with it and hopefully not be driven by it."

The professor's frankness provoked the class. One of them said, "But isn't the whole point of counseling, after diagnosing and naming the ailment, to help relieve suffering? And what causes more suffering than our inability to love and forgive those who've wounded us?"

That touched off an intense exchange. One student summarized what many of us were thinking: "It's not that I expect problems to be instantly eliminated. Forgiving is a process. But is the most we can hope merely the ability to name and understand our problems? Can't we ever be healed too? Isn't loving and forgiving a better way of living than not merely being controlled by anger? If that's the case, how do we help our clients find the power to change?"

The professor responded, "What we're attempting to do is to enable our patients to understand their true hidden feelings, to bring them to the surface and to experience them for what they are. So don't force your values or neurosis about forgiveness onto the patient!"

I raised my hand again and said, "I'd like to make three observations. First, I agree completely that there will be no progress until we understand and experience our real feelings. But having done that, how do we keep those feelings from destroying us? Isn't that why some of us have this 'neurosis' about seeking to forgive? The man needed to see he had more than a professed love for his mother. But after he's uncovered and identified his hostility, how does he keep it from devouring him? Surely the answer isn't to pretend he doesn't feel hate or that his mother is perfect. How can he be honest about his real feelings and yet get beyond them? Second, I wonder if you feel the words 'love your enemy' are rooted in neurosis. And third, I'd like to say that I'm *not* taking this course for credit."

The class exploded into laughter, and the teacher, smiling, but with more candor than he may have realized, said, "If you guys are looking for a changed heart, I think you're looking in the wrong department."

But the truth is, we *are* looking for a changed heart. We have seen that there can be no positive growth where there is pretense, no solution until we identify and own our problem. We have observed that robust living is more than the identification of problems. After we see we need to change, how do we find the power to do it? If the cross enables us to see our problem and how God has solved it, then the resurrection is where we see whether human behavior can be changed, and if so, how.

Celebration Sunday

There is nothing quite like the joy with which Christians celebrate Easter. What is it about Easter that causes believers to celebrate with such irrepressible joy, whether in Washington, San Francisco, Seoul or Sydney? For a start, Christ came. He visited planet earth like a meteor from outer space that struck with such an impact that the world has never been the same since. But that was only the beginning. When the worst our world could muster—death—was brought down on him, he rose from the dead. Yes, he blasted it open, brushed it aside, and now the entire universe will never be the same. Where once it was a claustrophobic death-locked cell, a gaping hole for freedom has been torn by the resurrection. Those two events, the crucifixion and the resurrection of Jesus, have changed everything.

It's easy to be blasé about Christ's visit to planet earth, even on a purely historical plane. It is easy to become parochial in our view of Jesus, as if the Christian faith were a cult that sprang up in Fresno. We forget that the Christian faith was first embraced by Jews, not by Gentiles, that its origins were Eastern, not Western. The question most asked in the generation after Jesus died was, Can I as a Gentile believe in Jesus? Now the question asked by modern Jews is, How could I as a Jew believe in Jesus? We have somehow come full circle.

Just consider some of the ways Christ has made a difference on our planet. Much of the world measures time from the moment of his birth. Literature, art and music have all drawn from his life. Imagine Bach, Handel and Mozart without the inspiration or the themes drawn from the life of Jesus. When we look at the height to which the human spirit has soared through the arts, we might wonder whether it has ever risen higher than in response to Jesus' presence on earth. Whether we follow Jesus or not, his coming has made a difference everywhere.

Anyone for Breakfast?

For someone who was to have such a stunning impact on history, Jesus' first appearances after the resurrection were remarkably simple and unobtrusive. If I had risen from the dead, I would have done it right! I would have rented the Roman Coliseum, hired the Royal Philharmonic, secured a Hollywood producer and put on a show the likes of which no one has ever seen. Yet that is not the way he did it. In one account, Peter is in a boat on Lake Galilee and sees Jesus on the shore. In his joy, Peter jumps out of the boat and starts swimming to shore. And what is the risen Lord doing on one of these first mornings of this glorious supernatural era? He is making Peter breakfast.

Somehow we expect a little more of a postresurrection appearance! But here is Jesus, risen from the dead and saying something like "How would you like your eggs?" Jesus does not put on a show, but he does transform lives. The one constant in all the resurrection appearances is that no life is the same after seeing Jesus alive.

Then there is the appearance back in Jerusalem. Putting together the accounts of Luke and John, we learn that because of fear of their fellow Jews, Jesus' followers had locked and barred themselves in a room. We can imagine the little band of disciples huddled together in fear in this dimly lit room, their leader gone, uncertain of the future, confused and not knowing what the next step should be. Suddenly Jesus is standing among them. Those walls of thick stone could not keep him out. He says, "Peace be with you"—*Shalom alekhem*, a familiar greeting that is used in Israel even today. But the terrified disciples thought they were seeing a ghost. So how does Jesus convince them that it is truly he?

If God had wanted, he could have let them know that Jesus had risen in a much more supernatural way. There could have been a mighty rush of wind and a great tremor. They would have turned to one another and said, "Did you feel that? I think he has risen!"

What actually happened could not have been more ordinary. In Luke's account we are told that Jesus appeals to their physical senses. He tells them, "You can see me, hear me, touch me." When the disciples still do not believe, Jesus asks them for fish. He then eats the fish and asks them, "Could a ghost eat a fish?" Does that sound spectacular enough? If not something cosmic, we would at least expect a blessing or *something* religious. No wonder, Luke tells us, they disbelieved for joy (see Luke 24:41). It was just too good to be true. Words simply couldn't be found to express the awe that must have pervaded that room.

It was probably by the grace of God, too, that Jesus ate fish and not bread. After he had left, the disciples no doubt questioned whether they had really seen anyone. If he had eaten bread, they would have probably concluded later that while they *thought* they had brought five loaves, they had actually only brought four. But Jesus ate the fish. It is not hard to imagine the disciples picking up his leftover fish bones later and saying, "I *know* there was fish on those bones when we came into this room!"

The Fellowship of the Wounded

John's account of the same story of the upper room adds three significant details. Presumably after Jesus has eaten the fish and was well into the conversation, he says a second time, "Peace be with you!" (John 20:21). He then shows them his wounds, commissions them and empowers them to go out into the world as he has been sent. These acts are linked, and each sheds light on the meaning of the resurrection.

To understand what Jesus was doing, we need to remember what wounds represent. Wounds are evidence of suffering. Wounds reveal the injuries that result from being bruised, lacerated or broken, whether physically or emotionally.

What do *our* human wounds represent? In his book on marriage, *Getting the Love You Want*, Harville Hendrix writes that to be human is to be wounded.[1] All of us are a storehouse of unmet childhood needs, of unfulfilled desires to be nurtured and protected. Consequently, as adults, some of us tend to cling to people out of a need for attachment, perhaps because we did not get to spend enough time in a parent's lap. Others of us keep people at a distance, perhaps because we felt engulfed or because our parents rejected us. Hendrix's thesis is that "fusers" (people with a great need for attachment) tend to marry "alienators" (people who need some distance from others).

But looking for the root of these behaviors does not mean that we put all the blame on our parents. It is simply stating a truth that because we live in a broken world, all of us are wounded people, raised by wounded parents, who marry wounded spouses and who wound our children. We certainly do not wish to continue the cycle, but we will nonetheless. We may cover our scars as best we can, whether through denial or bravado. But the scars remain. Indeed, Hendrix believes that it is in the context of intimate relationships, especially marriage, that our deepest wounds are revealed.

Ours is an age when psychology tends to eat up theology, so we need to underscore for ourselves that there are more than psychological reasons for our wounds. As has been stressed throughout this book, the ultimate source of human woundedness comes from the dislocations of not making God the center of our lives. Having put ourselves out of joint with God, we have wounded ourselves.

But when we turn to consider Jesus, that train of thought stops short. His wounds are different. Jesus knew sorrow, pain, frustration and exasperation as we do. But until the cross, he never experienced the separation from God that is the result of sin. That, far more than the nails and the suffocation, is why the cross was so excruciating. That is why Jesus couldn't go off to death singing hymns as the later martyrs did. That is why even Socrates seems more upbeat in handling death than Jesus. Jesus alone knew what it was to pay the price for human sin and experience the utter anguish and abandonment of separation from God. That is what hell is, and hell is what Jesus' agony was about. He who had never known a moment apart from the presence of his Father was willing to be severed from him and actually *become* sin for us.

So the wounds that Jesus showed to the disciples were different. They represented his suffering and death on the cross, his gift of love. When Jesus showed them, he didn't say, "Well, it goes to show that time really does heal all wounds." He simply says, "Peace be with you." He had already spoken this greeting when he entered the room, so it seems odd that he would repeat it. He probably never intended it to be simply a conventional greeting the first time, but it certainly isn't the second time as Jesus repeats the greeting and shows them his wounds.[2]

Dr. Cheryle Brown, a biblical scholar and good friend, believes that Jesus is referring to what had been written earlier of the suffering servant in Isaiah 53. He is telling them that he is the literal fulfillment of that text: "But he was pierced for our transgressions, he was crushed for our iniquities; the punishment that brought us *peace* was upon him, and by his wounds we are healed. We all, like sheep, have gone astray, each of us has turned to his own way; and the LORD has laid on him the iniquity of us all" (Isaiah 53:5-6, emphasis mine).

Thus the resurrection and those freshly healing wounds are the proof that God has accepted Jesus' sacrifice for us. In a way that we can never fully grasp, God has transformed the wounds of Jesus into something that brings life, healing and wholeness to *us*, the broken, wounded and suffering. His death-wounds are our life. "By his wounds we are healed." It will always remain the world's last mystery how the death of God's Son can make sick people well, sinful people forgiven and suffering people healed. But that is the wonder of the cross, and even in the dawn-fresh glory of the resurrection its marks are evident.

The Effect of Jesus' Resurrection on Us

Just as Jesus came to the disciples, so he comes to us behind our locked doors of fear and confusion. We too carry scars and have been wounded. We too feel trapped by sin and failure. And Jesus comes to us, shows us his wounds, and says, "Accept my gift of peace." It is real peace he is offering, because through his wounds we can be reconciled to God. He gives us hope and peace and joy through the transforming power of the resurrection. He does not eliminate our suffering, but he does transform it and gives us cause to have hope despite our woundedness.

It would be very difficult to trust a God who had not suffered, who didn't know what sorrow is. But what we see is the "man of sorrows," God's Son, boldly, unashamedly showing his scars and speaking words of peace.

As the writer to the Hebrews says, "For we do not have a high priest who is unable to sympathize with our weaknesses, but we have one who has been tempted in every way, just as we are—yet was without sin. Let us then approach the throne of grace with confidence, so that we may receive mercy and find grace to help us in our time of need" (Hebrews 4:15-16).

Jesus' resurrection scars also prepare us for the fact that there may be pain in our life too. There may come a time when little makes sense, and evil and chaos seem to be winning the day. These may be times when we feel hopelessness and confusion, when we do not see even a flicker of light. And the lesson of Jesus' scars is to hold on, to be patient and trust God, even when we cannot see any reason to do so. He will help us. He may not take away the suffering, but he will walk with us through it. And that alone has the power to transform us. How can we be sure? Because the joy of the resurrection was preceded by the agony of Good Friday.

The cross gives us perspective on our pain. As much as it hurts, we know at the deepest level that it is going to be all right. There is a loving God who can sustain us, enable us to endure and mold us into someone better than we were before. The cross prepares us for the difficult times. The resurrection proves that God is greater than evil, and it gives us confidence and hope during the dark times. Because the risen Christ's wounds show us that our hope is not in vain.

The Very Same Power

Imagine yourself back at Jesus' crucifixion and burial. Imagine you were able to sneak into the garden tomb. You are alone with the corpse of Jesus. What do you feel? Fear, perhaps. You are a follower of Jesus and they killed him, so will they do the same to you? You feel anger, not only at those who crucified him but also at Jesus. Why did he insist on dying? Why did he choose this senseless strategy? He could have withdrawn for a while and let things cool off. Any idiot could have escaped the guards. When they arrived to arrest him and saw him, they fell down! It would have been easy to have bolted. But Jesus *deliberately* gave himself over to them. And now look at him; his cause is as dead as his corpse. You saw him perform miracles, set your heart on fire with truth, give you hope and purpose as you had never known it before. And now he lies there, still and cold, unable to help anyone.

But wait—you start when suddenly you hear something move. It's dark, and you assume it is your imagination. Then you think you hear someone breathing. You summon all the courage you can muster and turn around to face what is there. And it's Jesus, risen, standing, radiant, stretching out his hand toward you. You respond as most of the disciples did in the resurrection appearances: in modern jargon, you flip out!

And here is what is only a little less startling than that. The very same power that raised Jesus from the dead, that made the amino acids rekindle and the corpse sit up, that revitalized dead cells and restored breath to empty lungs, is the power that is given to us when we receive Christ. Everything about the resurrection speaks of empowered newness. As Eugene Peterson writes, "The Bible is not a script for a funeral service, but it is the record of God always bringing life where we expected to find death. Everywhere it is the story of resurrection."[3]

I'm always amazed that some religious people have such a romance with the past. We hear of *The Old-Time Gospel Hour* and "Gimme That Old-Time Religion" and so forth. There is no such romance in the New Testament. With the past forgiven and the future opened with a cross-shaped hole blasted through the grave, the stress is on the present as it stretches through the future into eternity.

The resurrection enables us to live differently because we are given something permanently that we did not have before. The agent of our transformation and the One who enlivens us day by day as we grow in God is his Holy Spirit. Because we have been united to Christ in a living, vital way, we receive life and power through the Spirit.

Beyond Happiness to Joy

Let's pick up that theme of empowered newness and think how the resurrection affects our journey and our search. Take Thomas Jefferson's "pursuit of happiness," or what we earlier recognized as the human desire to be happy and to be loved. Some say the longing is misplaced, since we live in a fallen world and even the deepest happiness is transient. As they point out rightly, the word *happiness* has the root *hap*—which means "chance." Happiness is inevitably chancy because it is dependent on happenstance. All sorts of things can undermine happiness—time, change and tragedy above all. There isn't anything intrinsically wrong with happiness, but trying to build on just the right set of circumstances is seeking too insecure a base.

All that is correct, but the Bible's answer is unexpected. Happiness is emphatically not enough. The answer is not to reject happiness, it is to go beyond it to joy. That is what Jesus offers. "I have told you this so that my joy may be in you and that your joy may be complete" (John 15:11). Yes! God wants even more for us than our deepest desire. Joy is different from happiness because of the ultimacy of its fulfillment and because it is a profound reality regardless of our circumstances. Rooted in God, empowered by the energies of the resurrection, joy does not depend on getting the right income, the perfect spouse, the right mix of things. Joy goes so far beyond happiness that it is present even in the midst of deep unhappiness. Corrie ten Boom was a Dutch woman whose family was sent to a Nazi concentration camp for hiding Jews in their home during World War II. In her book *The Hiding Place* she recounts that while she certainly did not feel "happy" to be in Ravensbruck, she did experience joy.

Beyond Insecurity to Love

A good example of our empowered newness is seen in how God meets our need to be loved. The resurrection shows that we are more than flesh and blood. We are created to be filled with the very Spirit of God. It is contact with the love of God that addresses our longing for love, our problem of insecurity, and fills our emptiness. He is what our hearts have longed for unawares. God receives us as we are, and he loves us fully and freely. Finally we discover the love we ached for, which is totally dependable, which knows us intimately and loves us fully.

Surprisingly, our yearnings for sex and romance often closely parallel our yearning for God. Earlier I alluded to two women who had been disappointed in romance. Both wanted to obliterate their symptoms. My first friend wanted to die to the idea of romantic love, while the friend having the affair with a married man went even further.

"Sex is evil. All it's there for is to get us into trouble and lead us into bondage. I thought when I became a Christian my drives would go away. It just shows how unspiritual I am that I'm still so sexual."

"You can no more cease being sexual than you can cease breathing. And who said becoming a Christian makes you dry up sexually?" I asked.

"But sex just leads to addiction, so I've got to stop being sexual."

"No, you've got to stop the *addiction*. You'll never cease being sexual. Your problem is you think all of your problem is sexual. What is it that you hunger for? Surely part of it is the longing for nurture and intimacy. But there's a deeper hunger for God that you've ignored. I understand why you've used an affair to fill the void. Romantic love and sexual fulfillment are so close to what we want, and it's much easier to get a quick fix that momentarily fills our longing than to go to God."

"Look, Becky, I need a man who will hold me. I just don't think God is enough. You are right, I want sex, I want love, I want nurture. So don't try to fool me that God and prayer can satisfy my longing," she said.

"But you've had sex—lots of it. If sex or romantic love were the complete answer, you wouldn't be in the mess you're in. I'm not saying all you need is God. What I am telling you is you're starving to death in one area and transferring all of your needs, even your need for God, into another area. And the more feverishly you demand that this area meet all your needs, the greater your hunger and torment are. You're saying you're only made of the earth. I'm saying you're made of heaven too."

What these women want is what we all want. We want to be nourished, understood and loved to the core of our being. We long for intimacy and to feel bonded. We need a vast range of affectionate human contacts. But we're still left feeling only partially filled. Why? Why isn't human love enough?

The resurrection shows us that we are more than emotional and physical beings, we are also spiritual beings who need God. Our emptiness is real. Our desire for love is deep. But our deepest longing of all is for God.

As C. S. Lewis writes, "We should hardly dare to ask that any notice be taken of ourselves. But we pine. The sense that in this universe we are treated as strangers, the longing to be acknowledged, to meet with some response, to bridge some chasm that yawns between us and reality, is part of the inconsolable secret." What the Bible reveals is that

> our life-long nostalgia, our longing to be reunited with something in the uni-
> verse from which we now feel cut off, to be on the inside of some door which
> we have always seen from the outside, is no mere neurotic fantasy, but the
> truest index of our real situation. And to be at last summoned inside would
> be both glory and honor beyond all of our merits and also the healing of that
> old ache.[4]

But to find God, to pray, to worship, isn't easy. Peterson muses, "Because
it is so difficult we are always ready to go for something easier, especially if
that something seems to include all the essentials of worship."[5] And that is
what romance and sex promise—to fill our need for love and to enable us
to be lost in something larger than we are.

"Because I longed for eternal life, I went to bed with harlots and drank
for nights on end. . . . I soared in bliss . . . but awoke with the bitter taste of
the mortal state," Clamence said. Sacrilege! we say. How can anyone han-
kering for eternal life end up with a whore? More easily than we might
think. The longing for eternal life springs from the realization of our
incompleteness. And our incompleteness makes us long for fusion, for
ecstasy and for intimacy. Because our romantic yearnings so closely mirror
what our spirits seem to be missing, we get easily sidetracked.

What went wrong with Clamence's quest to fill his great longing through
romance and sex? He was using them as a substitute for God. It was worship gone wrong. His evil was not just sexual immorality but spiritual sacrilege. The secret unlocked in the Bible and revealed vividly through the
resurrection is that the love we seek so desperately in the flesh can *ultimately* only be satisfied in the spirit. Indeed, the more ferociously we try to
fill our need in our own way, the more frustrated we will become and the
more likely it will become an obsession, creating an even deeper hunger
than we had in the first place.

We must be honest here. Since to be human is to experience unmet
needs to a degree, aren't we just projecting those unmet needs onto our
relationship with God? Is God merely our Great Compensation in the
Sky? It is true that we project onto God a great deal of ourselves, includ-

ing our emotional needs. Indeed the Scriptures encourage us to do so. The mystery is not that we do it but how well it works; that the love of God can fill us, sustain us and meet our needs so richly.

I sometimes wonder if this truth isn't lost on Christians. When I told a Christian friend about my two friends whose love lives were in turmoil (being careful to shield their identities), her response was "Well, it's clear they're going to have to learn obedience!"

There is a sense in which she is right, of course. All of us need to be resolute in departing from what destroys us and to be willing to face some empty times before the rewards of obedience become a reality. But my friends need more than cold and mechanical obedience. They need to experience God's presence, the gentle breeze of his loving touch on their lives. When the modern church preaches a severe obedience, it becomes even harder for those who are trapped and sinking. It feels to them that there is no payoff. Better to fill themselves with destructive things and still feel partially full, they think, than to follow God and feel empty.

We are not after mechanical self-denial any more than blatant self-indulgence. Rather, we seek obedience based on an increasing awareness of and trust in the Father's love. Obedience may *begin* somewhat mechanically, making us feel inwardly barren at first. But it leads us to peace and joy. The answer to someone who has been filling self with destructive things (which often are good gifts gone awry) is not to say, "Quit filling yourself with bad things!" but rather, "Get away from what is destroying you and fill your inner being with God himself. He is what your heart has hungered for all along."

I was heartened by another woman's response to these stories. She has a wonderful marriage and no catastrophic problems, but she said, "I know exactly what these women are longing for. Even in the best of marriages, or in the most fulfilled lives, there is still an emptiness that only God can fill. If we don't allow God to have access to our deepest selves, if we don't allow him to be our center, and we merely coast on whatever contentment we may have, we'll end up mediocre Christians without passion or fire. We'll look at the needy in our midst with puzzlement, not compassion, because our own experience with God is so superficial."

That's easy for her to say, my friends would likely respond. But she is talking about knowing God out of richness and fullness, not the emptiness we are facing. It is true. Some people have never been loved in the way they long for. There are people who have to live with an open wound. Yet Christianity never pretended differently. "It also remains true, however, that there is a divine love, which, if we are open to it, reaches us in many ways, expected and unexpected. It may not come in the form we have been looking for, but in one way or another, God's love reaches us."[6] And the offer of his love that fills us and heals us is the result of the resurrection.

> Indeed if we consider the unblushing promises of reward and the staggering nature of the rewards promised in the Gospels, it would seem that Our Lord finds our desires not so strong, but too weak. We are half-hearted creatures, fooling around with drink and sex and ambition when infinite joy is offered us, like an ignorant child who wants to go on making mud pies in a slum because he cannot imagine what is meant by the offer of a holiday at the sea. We are far too easily pleased.[7]

Holding the Tension

Mention of the joy in unhappiness or the barren times of obedience as we slowly learn to trust in God's love is a reminder of the extraordinary realism and balance of the Bible. We're not called to joy alone, and certainly not to unhappiness alone, but to joy *in the midst of* unhappiness. That is especially vital with the resurrection, because it's easy to get carried away by it. It's true that we are no longer what we were. But it's also true that we are not yet what we will be. We are living "between the times" of what we are now and what we will be when Christ returns. Even the resurrection power we know now is but the first sample of what is to come. Let me illustrate the need for balance by telling stories about two friends.

The first is Henry, a delightful friend whose life is marked by genuine joy and enthusiasm for God. He has taught me a great deal about the importance of praise and adoration. But Henry once came into our home irate that a service station attendant had treated him with contempt and indifference.

"You wouldn't believe the attitude of the man at the station!" he said.

"He was rude and obnoxious!" I told him I knew just the guy he was referring to and agreed that he did have a foul attitude.

"Well," he said, "I don't have to put up with that. I told him that I would not receive his spirit of hostility, and I drove off! How dare he treat me that way? He simply can't get away with it!"

"Why not?" I asked.

"Because I belong to Christ!" he snapped back.

"Well, in light of what they did to Jesus, I'd say you got off pretty lucky. And don't I detect a bit of anger in you?" I asked.

Now Henry has a disciplined prayer life. He has seen thrilling answers to prayer and great spiritual victories. He is full of thanksgiving, and it truly comes from the heart. Yet in far more serious encounters than that one, I rarely hear him acknowledge sin. I can't ever recall his admitting something was his fault. Doubtless his responses reflect his character, but they are also shaped by certain underlying theological assumptions, perhaps unbeknownst to him.

Henry focuses heavily on the meaning and benefits of the resurrection and little on the cross. This approach emphasizes our newness in Christ but forgets the old nature. It emphasizes our transformation but not our continued sinfulness. It emphasizes the "no longer" but ignores the "not yet." Those who embrace this emphasis are correct in their refusal to allow sin to be what defines them. It is our transformed identity in Christ, not sin, that defines what it means to be truly human. Their mistake, however, is in assuming that our new and true self is so transformed that it is almost beyond sin. But to not perceive sin as much of a menace is to open the door to denial all over again. Sin is so devious that it would gladly have us emphasize praise at the expense of repentance so it can remain hidden.

My second friend, Sheila, is equally devout and sincere in her love for God. But the thrust of her daily press release is "Well, I blew it again. I'm such a rotten sinner. But what can I do? The heart is deceitful and wicked. And my motives are always so complex. How can God even put up with me? If you want to know who I am just look at my sins. Two steps forwards, ten steps back—that's me."

Sheila plays Tweedledee to Henry's Tweedledum. In all her attitudes she ignores what Henry stresses, and stresses what he ignores. He goes for the resurrection; she for the cross. He thinks of the "no longer;" she of the "not yet." He sees the glass half full; she half empty. Worst of all, she allows sin, which never reveals humanity as God intends, to be what defines her.

The more I listen to her, the more I wonder, where are the joy, the freedom and the victory that is ours in Christ? Sheila's version of spiritual identity almost sounds like a borderline character disorder! She gives the impression that everything depends on her obedience. Our human responsibility *is* vitally important, but Sheila makes little mention of the power of grace that transforms us. She is more taken up with sin.

What can we learn from Henry and Sheila? The challenge of practicing biblical truths in a fallen world is holding the tension, keeping the balance. The resurrection provides decisively for substantial, radical change, here and now. But the presence of sin means an unrelenting battle that will not be over until Christ comes again. An African brother said it all. When I asked him how he was, he answered jubilantly with a glistening smile, "Repenting and rejoicing, sister!"

Does testifying to the power of the resurrection in our lives mean we can speak only when there are victories and success? Or can we speak of God's power and presence even in the midst of catastrophic circumstances? We must remember that Jesus told his disciples, "As the Father has sent me, I am sending you" (John 20:21). How was Jesus sent? He was sent to suffer with a suffering world by identifying in love so deeply that he was even willing to die for us. He sends us out as healers, but still in the process of being healed ourselves.

We are sent as people who have experienced brokenness and woundedness yet who also know something of the life-giving, transforming power of the resurrection in our lives. And though we have not arrived, we are definitely on our way, and in this we rejoice.

The truth is people are eager to listen when they know that we suffer and struggle as they do, yet God is giving us the strength to take the next step and go on one more day. People can tell when the word of peace we speak has come through the fire of our own lives. There is something *powerful* in a witness like that.

Most people want to know if God really makes a difference. Can Jesus help them and give meaning and purpose and guidance and strength to their lives too? When our answer is "Yes, I have experienced firsthand God's power in the midst of pain" we give others hope. God will take our wounds and use them to minister to the similarly wounded. We are sent out as wounded healers; people who are allowing their transformed wounds to be used by God for his glory.

One day I was speaking to a conference of wealthy, upper-class women. The woman who introduced me was striking—impeccably attired, gracious, lovely. My topic was sin, and as she was introducing me I recall thinking, *I know this doctrine is universally true, but it's hard to believe it when everyone here looks so perfect and together.* I felt sure that this woman in particular would not have a clue about what I was about to say.

When I finished speaking, she stood up to direct us to lunch. But first she said, "What Becky has been telling us about sin and our problem of denial has moved me deeply. And I have decided to share something with you. As most of you know, we have sent our daughter to the finest European boarding schools. That sounds very glamorous and successful. But what you don't know, and what I only recently have accepted as reality, is that my daughter is a serious drug addict.

"Three weeks before Christmas, I finally came to see that all of the finest schools in the world would not take away her addiction. We have placed her in a rehabilitation center, and twice a week my husband and I fly to the center. We are going through a program called Al-Anon. And part of my recovery is being able to admit this to you now.

"This is the first time I have ever told anyone. I thought my apprehension was that I wanted to protect my daughter's reputation in your eyes. That is part of it. But I now see that it is more than that. I wanted to protect *my* reputation. What I need to tell you is that I am not the perfect mother; I do not have the perfect Christian home. We have serious problems and we are not out of the woods. Yet I can also tell you that God has never been more real to me; he has given me peace in the midst of great trauma, hope in the midst of great suffering and strength to go on to the next day. I know, as never before, that my Redeemer liveth."

She sat down, and no one moved or spoke for the first moment. Then very quietly, I saw the women turn to those around them and begin to talk deeply about the pain in their own lives. I suddenly saw tissues come out of purses and tears roll down faces. That woman had testified to the power of the resurrection at the point of her wounds, and she deeply ministered God's hope.

Becoming a Resurrection Person

Living out the New Way will shape everything about us. It will slowly transform our values, our attitudes, our perception of self and others. The reality of our new life with Christ must begin to seep into our consciousness and penetrate everything we do. Flannery O'Connor's mean-spirited, unregenerate character, the misfit in "A Good Man Is Hard to Find," understands this when he says the trouble with Jesus is that "He thrown everything off balance."[8] That is absolutely right. To follow Jesus is to be influenced by a totally new angle that will seem anathema to most others. We will be living off balance from the norm. How does this change translate into practical reality?

During an out-of-town speaking engagement, I was staying in the home of a woman I will call Catherine. I asked her how she came to faith. She said she had a not-very-devout Episcopalian background and went to church on holidays, but faith had not been a personal issue for her. Slowly she had begun to feel that something was missing from her life. Materially she had everything she could wish for, yet she felt an undefined emptiness.

At the same time she began to notice there was something remarkable about her maid, Ruby. Ruby had been coming to her home for ten years; she was part of the family. Ruby always radiated a calm and joy that Catherine envied. She noticed that Ruby sang hymns while she washed the kitchen floors. Why would *anyone* want to sing when they did something as menial as wash a floor? The more Catherine observed her behavior, the more intrigued she became; she wanted to know the source of Ruby's peace. So she asked Ruby to tell her the secret of her contentment, and Ruby shared her faith. Eventually Catherine decided to be a follower of Jesus too. But the part of the story that really struck me was to follow.

Suddenly Catherine began to have trouble with her teenage daughter. The police called to inform her that her daughter had been arrested for breaking into a neighbor's home and stealing jewelry. She had cocaine in her purse when they arrested her. Catherine came back from the county jail devastated and weeping. She began to tell Ruby what had happened.

"Ruby, what am I going to do? How can I help her? It may be too late! I am absolutely distraught," she sobbed.

Ruby said, "Child, Jesus already died for your daughter; there's no need for you to die too."

"But Ruby," Catherine protested, "you don't understand. I have prayed for her and nothing has happened."

"And how long have you been praying for your child?" Ruby asked.

"For at least six months, ever since I came to faith," Catherine answered.

"And how long have I been working for you?" Ruby asked.

"Ten years," Catherine answered.

"That's right! And for nine years and six months I was on my knees washing these floors and praying for the salvation of this home! And did you hear me complain because it took so long? Don't you rush Jesus, girl! You give him room, be patient, and pray!"

"Well, I try to pray, but I don't feel like anything happens," Catherine answered.

"You call that piddly stuff I hear you do prayin'?" Ruby asked.

"But Ruby, you don't understand, I am desperate!" Catherine pleaded.

"Now we're talkin' prayer! You let Ruby teach you how to pray. The cleaning can wait. Do you have a Bible?" Ruby asked.

Now Catherine was puzzled because she knew that Ruby couldn't read. She quickly got a Bible, although she was afraid that Ruby might feel embarrassed. But to her surprise, Ruby began walking around the house and lifted her arms and prayed the psalms in her beautiful deep voice, word for word. Her voice crescendoed: "He who dwells in the shelter of the Most High, who abides in the shadow of the Almighty, will say to the Lord, 'My refuge and my fortress; my God, in whom I will trust.'" She would turn to Catherine and tell her which psalm she was quoting, and then she was off on another one. Picture the scene: Ruby calmly, jubilantly striding through the house as she prayed, Catherine frantically trying to keep up with her.

The next day as I was leaving, Ruby came in, having just arrived by bus. We spoke in the living room, and I told her how moved I was by her influence in that home. "Oh, Becky, if you only knew how I have *grieved* for the poverty in this home!" Ruby said, as I sat and listened amidst Baccarat crystal, Persian rugs and priceless antiques.

That is the difference the resurrection makes. That is how Jesus has "thrown everything off balance." Jesus turns everything upside down. For who would have guessed, walking into that home for the first time, who was the teacher and who the student, who was the literate and who the illiterate, who was the wealthy and who the poor?

Following Jesus is living life from a new angle, living life with a new energy resource. And the different angle and power he offers have been opened up by the resurrection. We can become "resurrection people" like Ruby. Ruby's last words as I left were "But Jesus is winnin' and there's a new song to sing." A new song to sing indeed.

8

How Do
We Change?

What else can save us but your hand
remaking what you have made?
AUGUSTINE OF HIPPO

I once heard a story of two preachers. One was a gifted and well-known expositor. When he preached, people came from all over and crowded the church to hear him. But whenever he had a free Sunday, he always went to hear an obscure country preacher few people knew. One day somebody said to him, "Why is it that someone as famous as you goes to hear an unknown country preacher on your free Sundays?"

He said, "Well, you see, when I preach they sit on top of the confessional. When he preaches we all walk into it."

This book has been a journey toward a moment of truth. But when we arrive, what does it mean to confess, and how do we do it? We have seen that there is something seriously wrong with us. We have seen the extravagant measures that God has taken to rescue us. We have seen his power to change and restore us. But how do we incorporate all of this into our lives? How do we get on board the train?

The Little Step Without Which There Are No More
The Gospel of Luke opens with the announcement that Jesus is coming.
John the Baptist, we are told, is the royal herald sent ahead to prepare us for
his arrival. And according to John, the only way to prepare is by *repenting,* a
word that in Greek means to "turn around" and so to have a total change of
heart and mind. Without repentance there is no way for Christ to come
into our lives and effect the new start and the complete change. As C. S.
Lewis points out, repentance is not something God demands of you before
he will take you back and which he could let you off if he chose; it is simply
a description of what going back is like.

In one of his great silent films, Charlie Chaplin plays a prisoner being
transported on a boat that has shipwrecked. The film begins with Chaplin
alone on the beach looking at a fetter around his leg attached to a ball and
chain. He is unable to get free. The entire film deals with his relationship to
this ball and chain in the sand, as we see him trying to figure out how to
escape from its weight. First he thinks, *I know what I'll do—I'll humor it! I
will amuse it, and when its guard is down, I'll dash away.* He makes little jokes,
trying to amuse the ball and chain until he feels he has accomplished his
purpose. Then he walks the length of the chain and *bam!* Down he goes in
the sand.

He scratches his head, wondering what to do next. Then he decides: *I
will trick it! I will outsmart it.* So he tries to outsmart and trick the ball and
chain. He gets up and walks the length of the chain and *bam!* Down he goes
into the sand again.

This time he gets up and walks back more thoughtfully. His next strategy is reason. *I know. I will talk to it! I will reason with it.* He talks to the ball
and chain until he believes he has convinced it to let go. He then walks the
length of the chain. *Bam!* Down he goes again, into the sand.

By now, of course, he's coming to the end of his patience. So he employs
a final strategy. He ignores the ball and chain. He tries to pretend it is not
there. We see him kicking sand over it, and for a while it truly looks as if
the problem has vanished. Thinking he has finally solved the dilemma, he

strides the length of the chain. *Bam!* Down he goes.

At this point insight finally dawns. A light turns on in Chaplin's head: he realizes there is no way that he can solve his problem alone. If he is going to be helped, help will to have to come from the outside. For the first time we see him looking upward in the hope of seeing a plane or something that would signal hope of rescue.

The film is a parable of the human condition. Perhaps if we could see ourselves from the outside we'd look as comic as Charlie Chaplin. Our initial response when we have a problem is to say, "I can handle this, I can take care of it." And then we try every strategy possible. We argue, we wheedle, we turn a blind eye, we blame someone else, or we simply run away from dealing with it. We do anything to try to slip around the fact that we have a problem. But—if we are lucky—there usually comes a problem we cannot conquer by ourselves, that brings us to the point where we say, "This is beyond me. I'm stuck."

That is the point at which we become open to receiving the help that God longs to give us. To repent is to face up to our problem as well as the fact that we cannot do anything about solving it. One way the Bible describes repentance is as "coming to our senses"—clearly suggesting the madness of our trying to solve things on our own. That is what happened literally to Nebuchadnezzar, king of Babylon in the sixth century B.C. Nebuchadnezzar had lived like Clamence but with better reason—he really believed he was "master of the universe." After all, he was king. His royal word meant life or death for subjects throughout a vast empire. He was as God to them.

Finally, through combined illusion within and adulation without, he forgot that he was mortal, forgot that he was not divine, and went mad. Refusing to abandon his pride despite God's warnings, he was finally reduced to scrabbling on all fours like an animal. It was there, at the end of the line, that the spell of his illusions broke and he "came to his senses," acknowledging God and reality at once. In short, he repented.

Perhaps best of all, in the light of what we have looked at earlier, repentance reverses denial. We no longer hide from the truth, or need to. And it isn't just that the truth is inescapable: it's liberating. But it is at the point of repentance that we see that denial is not an invention of psychology. At its deepest, it is the diabolical face of sin. Long before psychology, the Bible said that sin means that we "suppress the truth in unrighteousness" (see Romans 1:18).

So when we repent, we reverse the process of denial. Prior to repentance, we project our best side and conceal our worst. But when we repent we turn this around. We reveal the worst to God, so that letting others see it is not the problem it was, because the worst has been forgiven. At the same time, we now conceal our "best." We do our best for God alone and no longer need to use it to gain the approval of others. Which is what Jesus means when he talks of doing one's good deeds in secret ("Do not let your left hand know what your right hand is doing," Matthew 6:3).

Confession—a Moment and a Way of Life
The first time we repent is often the worst and the best. It's the worst because the sin, pain and illusions are at their strongest. It's also the best because there's no joy in the world like the joy of having been freshly forgiven.

But repentance is not just a once-and-for-all experience of a moment. For those who come to know God, it's a way of life. It has to be, because sin and self are not easily displaced at the center of our lives. And, more important, our deepening desire for intimacy with God makes us more sensitive to sin, not less. So whether it is the new believer or the old, the meaning is the same. Repentance brought us to Christ in the first place, and repentance will keep on bringing us back.

Some believers seem to imagine that once they have come to know God, their walk with him will be uninterrupted bliss. While bliss is part of our life with God, indeed its goal, we can only attain it by confronting sin over and over as long as there is sin to confront, which will be until we see God face to face. If our expectation is that trusting God will make life easier because we won't have to deal with our dark side anymore, then we'll be discouraged and confused over and over again by the stubborn reality of sin.

Only after we get closer to God do we see our sinfulness with clarity. So the closer we get, the clearer sin becomes. Unless we remember this, we may even think our growing awareness of sin and our continued vulnerability to its temptation means that we are getting further from God. Then we fear that if Christ died for our sin, and we still battle with it, maybe we weren't really changed after all. But in fact the reverse is true. Our sensitivity to our sin indicates we are growing closer to God, not further away.

Unrepentance, of course, means the opposite. The further we are from God, the less aware we are of sin. In rarer cases, this can even mean that people seek to avoid sin in order to avoid God. The unrepentant Haze Motes in Flannery O'Connor's novel *Wise Blood* understands this: "There was a deep black wordless conviction in him, that the way to avoid Jesus was to avoid sin."[1]

Far more common is the way unrepentance leads to a numbing of sensitivity to sin, to human relationship and to God. This is what happened with the Nazi doctors interviewed by Robert J. Lifton. Such was their utter lack of moral confrontation, their refusal to admit their evil, he writes, that he was prevented from having any genuine relationship with them. Their lives were so built on the lie of their own innocence that any real intimacy with them was impossible.[2]

And if this is true of unrepentance on the human level, how much truer is it before God! To know God is to know the light of his presence. It is to know that there is nowhere left to hide. But to those beyond running, repentance means the promise of intimacy as well as the melting away of fear in the light of love.

Keeping Short Accounts

What are the practical steps we should take to repent, whether to establish a relationship with God for the first time or to restore a relationship that has been obstructed by unconfessed sin? Repentance is nothing if not specific and practical, and one of the most helpful pictures used to describe it is *keeping accounts*. For neglected sin is like mounting debt, and the secret of repentance is to keep those accounts short.

The first rule of repentance is that we must be timely and specific about the exact wrong we have done, whether in thought, word or deed. Are we doing this to let God in on the secret? No. The Bible tells us that God is the "heart knower." Everything is open before him. We are simply acknowledging what he already knows. Previously we tried to conceal our wrong because we could not face ourselves as we were. But now there is no longer any need to live in self-deception.

Is such confession psychologically unhealthy? On the contrary, there is a profound realism in the Bible's account of our inner turmoil when we refuse to acknowledge sin. The psalmist writes:

> When I kept silent,
>   my bones wasted away
>   through my groaning all day long.
> For day and night
>   your hand was heavy upon me;
> my strength was sapped
>   as in the heat of summer.
> Then I acknowledged my sin to you
>   and did not cover up my iniquity.
> I said, "I will confess
>   my transgressions to the LORD"—
> and you forgave
>   the guilt of my sin. (Psalm 32:3-5)

Simply to say, "God forgive me for all my sins. Amen," is neither adequate nor helpful. It isn't enough to say, "You know how boys will be boys." We must acknowledge our pride and exactly how we showed it; our need to be controlling and the people and situations where we tried it; we must mention the people we have hurt by name, and acknowledge what we did to them.

No Mere Regret

The second rule of repentance is to express genuine sorrow for what we have done. This is not to suggest mere regret, or self-flagellation and bitter remorse. The first is too weak and the others are both wrong. The Bible speaks of genuine or "godly sorrow," of being brokenhearted over the brokenness we have caused.

Maybe we know that we have sinned but frankly do not feel sorry about it. Then we can start by feeling sorrow over the fact that we feel no sorrow! We need to realize that part of the frightening reality of sin is that it numbs our conscience. Often what we call repentance is simply embarrassment that we've been caught. Our remorse is just shame at the consequences of our stupidity. In other words, we are not repenting of sin; we're regretting the pain that the sin has caused us. But if we "repent" only of the embarrassing and painful consequences of our sin, the sin will remain intact and will continue to exert power in our lives.

What is it, then, that we are to feel sorrow over? Isn't it that we have disobeyed God by settling for so much less than his highest, by giving ourselves to what is false and pushing him out? And those very choices and actions are what cost Jesus his life. Martin Luther was right: if our hearts do not tremble, then we of all people have reason to tremble.

> Let us now meditate on the passion of Christ. . . . The true contemplation is that in which the heart is crushed and the conscience smitten. Ponder the inexpressible and unendurable yearning that caused God's son to suffer in this way and you will tremble. And the more you ponder, the deeper will you tremble. Take this to heart and doubt not that you are the one who killed Christ. Your sins certainly did. And when you see the nails driven through his hands, be sure it is you that is pounding. . . . The whole value of the meditation on the suffering of Christ lies in this: that we should come to the knowledge of ourselves and think and tremble. And if you are so hardened that you do not tremble, then you of all people have reason to tremble. Pray to God that he will soften your heart.[3]

All Sin Is Sin Against God

The third rule of repentance is to confess our sin to God. But why should we confess to God if we have injured someone else? The answer is that the Creator of the universe has established a moral law, an absolute standard, and put it into our hearts. That law, Jesus tells us, can best be summarized thus: "Love the Lord your God with all your heart and with all your soul and with all your mind. . . . And . . . love your neighbor as yourself" (Matthew 22:37-38).

So even if our offense is against a neighbor whom we envied, or hated, or were unkind to, it is still a sin against God. Both we and our neighbor are God's, just as the commandment to love is his. God's law, planted in our very being, is something we "know" whether we believe in God or not. Therefore, regardless of what our sin is, the one to whom we primarily confess is God. That is what David acknowledged to God after he seduced Bathsheba and murdered her husband: "Against you, you only, have I sinned and done what is evil in your sight" (Psalm 51:4).

That does not mean that if we sin against our neighbor we have to confess only to God. By restricting confession we would be too easy on ourselves. As John Stott reminds us, "The confession must be made to the person against whom we have sinned and from whom we need and desire to receive forgiveness."[4] Alternatively, it would be just as wrong to go to the other extreme and widely publicize our confessions as a subtle form of egotism.

It is best to treat the sin that has been a secret in one's thoughts and heart as something to be confessed to God alone. What should be confessed to others are the sins we commit in word and deed. But all sins, however serious and whether known to others or not, must be confessed to God first. He sees them all:

O Lord, you have searched me
    and you know me.
You know when I sit and when I rise;
    you perceive my thoughts from afar.
You discern my going out and my lying down;
    you are familiar with all my ways.
Before a word is on my tongue
    you know it completely, O Lord. (Psalm 139:1-4)

Confession is sometimes hard on our pride, and we need to remember that we owe our pride nothing. At other times confession just doesn't seem to "work." We feel like saying, "But I have confessed my sin to God—I've confessed a thousand times and I can't find relief." Then it may be time to go to a trusted Christian friend and confess in that person's presence. We are to be God's go-betweens to one another. It is not that any one of us can forgive someone else. But when we find someone able to listen and pray with us for God's forgiveness, the barriers are broken through more easily. Even hearing that friend speak words of Scripture that pronounce God's forgiveness can be critical (Isaiah 1:18; 1 John 1:9).

Of course there is a danger—the friend may go out and tell others what we have said in confidence. Which is why we should choose only a mature and trusted friend. And never forget that someday we will be that friend to someone else. So if someone chooses you as a confessor, never say, "You did *what?*" Or "Reeeeally? Tell me some more!" But neither is it helpful to say, "That's no big deal. I did that last week." It is God's job, not ours, to make judgments. Our job is to listen, pray and seek, under the Holy Spirit, to be a midwife to the forgiveness and release that God is bringing to the one confessing.

The Ultimate U-Turn

The fourth rule of repentance is that we must change direction. As we saw, the meaning of the Greek work for repentance—*metanoia*—is changing direction, turning around, walking a different way. We don't uncover our sins just to have them forgiven, but so that we may forsake them. On that point, from that moment on, our behavior has to be resolutely and utterly different. Like old clothes, the old wrong ways have to be discarded. Whether what is wrong is a thought, a habit or an activity, repentance is always the prelude to deep, radical and lasting change, and it begins with a turnaround that is total.

These four rules by themselves could easily become mechanical, for a simple reason. They deal only with our part, and what makes forgiveness effective and a miracle is God's part. What does God do in response to all of this? First, he forgives us by wiping the slate absolutely clean. If we talk of sin and confession at a general level, we can skip into treating forgiveness lightly. God doesn't. With him there is no sense of "Oh, never mind, it doesn't matter." Sin does matter. The wrong we have done matters profoundly. It cost God the life of his Son for it to be wiped out and for us to be restored. So sacrifice is always present in forgiveness. Our forgiveness is precious precisely because it cost so much.

Again and again the Bible stresses the wonder that God is a forgiving God. He wants to deal with us tenderly, not harshly. His desire is to "blot out" our transgressions, to put them as far as the east is from the west, to bury them in the depths of the sea, to remember them no more. He has no choice but to pronounce judgment on sin, but his desire is never to condemn. The one who accuses, condemns and leaves us to die is the Evil One. God convicts so that we might see the truth, repent and be restored to life with him.

Born All Over Again

Next comes a surprising discovery: forgiveness is only the beginning. The second thing God gives us is new life, regenerating us by sending his Spirit to come live in us—something so revolutionary that Jesus uses the staggering image of being "born all over again."

The tragedy of sin is that it has ruined something that was created to be wonderful. God's image within us is a reminder that we have been created for something better than we are experiencing. Joe Cooke writes:

> I am like a beast in the trap. I was created to roam free, but sin has snapped its jaw around me and imprisoned me. I am like an eagle with a broken wing. God intended that I should fly high up in His blue heaven. But sin has broken me, and I cannot even get off the ground. I'm like a priceless violin created by a master. But the strings are broken and the pegs slip, and the wood is cracked. When the master tries to play me, he gets nothing out of me but a cacophonous wail.[5]

That is where the new life makes the difference. It may happen that after our initial zeal for God, we return to our old destructive patterns. Then our despair may be even greater. We will have had our hopes lifted only to discover that nothing has really changed. So we urgently need love and forgiveness, but even more we need *power* to become new people. If we are to have real hope, we must have hope of real change, and that change comes from the Spirit of God. As Lovelace Howard says, "It is the Spirit who empowers us to do what we could not do on our own, but what we must now do through his help."[6]

God's Spirit within us is what makes us a new creation. We now have within us our old human nature as well as God's new nature through his Spirit. Two distinct identities remain: the old and the new. We are not yet merged into one, but we are emphatically not the same as we were. As Paul reminded the new Christians in Corinth, "If anyone is in Christ, he is a new creation; the old has gone, the new has come!" (2 Corinthians 5:17). If through repentance and faith the new is fed and the old is starved, one will thrive and the other will wither until, by the power of God, a remarkably changed life will emerge. The reason we see so much compromise and hypocrisy in the lives of believers is failure to practice this radical repentance.

As Many Ways as There Are People

All of us come to God for different reasons and in different ways. There is only one constant. God responds to the human cry for help. All stories of conversions are different. Some are dramatic, others quiet. Some respond out of crisis, others in calm. But the common element to all is that one way or another, God reaches us. He comes though. He does not leave us alone. But neither does he barge in uninvited. God comes into our lives by our invitation only.

In the many years that I have been a Christian, I have seen many people turn their lives over to God and be changed. And yet the awesome mystery of conversion never fails to move me. Who can probe the inner workings of the heart and its reasons? Or if we know our own hearts, how can we convey their stories to one another? Yet conversion has been turned into a cliché for many, and for others it is the occasion for genuine fears.

For example, some fear that surrender to God means that they are too weak to stand on their own two feet. Is conversion for those who need something to get them through a moment of crisis? It is true that many people are converted during crisis, but the dynamic at work is not at all what some people think. It isn't that they have a momentary weakness in which they need help. Rather, it is in their experience of weakness that they see what has always been true, that a person without God is an incomplete person. To give up the pretense of a sufficiency we do not have in order to gain a sufficiency we cannot do without is about the costliest thing we can ever do—to our pride.

When I first came close to faith, I was afraid that if I surrendered my life to God he would take away my identity, or I'd become somewhat strange through the process. I simply could not imagine what a religious version of me would look like. Would I be required to race off to Bongo-Bongo as a missionary? Give up my love of jazz? Would I be required to act "religious" (as I understood it then) all the time? What would change and what would stay the same? Would God violate who I understood myself to be?

A related concern was whether my friends (none of whom were religious) would recognize me. My worst fear was that they would reject me as having become slightly demented. I could just hear them: "Too bad about Becky. She used to be so much fun."

In fact, my friends reinforced my fears. I remember discussing my quest with one of them who was highly skeptical. He had been dropped off at Sunday school as a child but had never regarded himself as religious. He was absolutely horrified at how serious I was. "Oh no, Becky, you're not going to start acting weird, are you?" he asked.

"Gosh, I don't think so," I responded.

"Yeah, but will you have to wear funny clothes or something?" he asked.

"Hey, I didn't say I was becoming a nun. I said that I may believe in God," I responded.

"I suppose that means you'll become a vegetarian?" he queried.

Now I was getting irritated. It sounded to me as if it would be better if I had confessed to a drug problem than a "religious problem." So I said, "Glad you brought that up. I've decided to stick to a diet of holy wafers and water for the time being. It feels right to me."

He took me seriously! In fact, in some perverse way it seemed to satisfy him, because it fed the stereotype that no one could be wholehearted in devotion to God and not be at least slightly kinky.

Still, I could not sort out what would happen to me in the process. Like Clamence, I knew my experience of life lacked something. There was an inner restlessness, an emptiness, a longing that never left me. I knew something was missing. But I was also afraid. Better to be an agnostic, I thought, and recognize a certain wistful empty space within, but still be "me," than give myself to God and wind up with no me at all.

Doubtless my fear that surrender to God would make me a little strange was fueled by my general impression of religious people. I must say that my view at this stage was largely a caricature. To be honest, I didn't know many religious people. But it was a caricature I believed as wholeheartedly as any creed. As I think back, I realize the believers I did meet during my searching days were a tremendous contrast to the stereotype in my mind. They were intelligent, articulate, well-read and—I cannot think of another word—normal! And since then I have found this to be more the norm than the exception. I did, however, meet a few who fit my worst preconceptions. They seemed pale and lifeless and almost fearful. They didn't engage in life with passion, intellect and zest. I have since realized that God loves all his children—the clingers as well as the movers and shakers. But in spite of the occasional poor example, what drove me to ask ultimate questions was my desire to know there was a foundation strong enough on which to base my life.

I looked into Hinduism, existentialism and several other philosophies. But not the Christian faith. I assumed I knew about that. After all, hadn't I been raised in America? I had even been a Girl Scout!

But whatever else I studied left me unsatisfied and frustrated. It wasn't that I was asking for absolute proof. That cannot be offered in most areas of life. I did want logical, defensible answers. I recall asking a believer how he knew his faith was true. "It's a feeling in my heart," he said.

"But what about your head?" I exclaimed. "I have a head as well as a heart!"

I dismissed people of faith, regardless of which brand they adhered to, as being sincere but only loosely rooted in reality. Rationality and faith struck me as mutually exclusive.

Then I stumbled across *Mere Christianity* by C. S. Lewis. In Lewis I found myself face to face with an intellect so disciplined, so lucid, so relentlessly logical, that all of my intellectual pride at not being a "mindless believer" was quickly squelched. I read Lewis line by line with a growing hunger. For the first time I realized that I did not know what biblical Christianity really was. How could I, when I had never read the Bible with a critical adult mind?

C. S. Lewis sparked my interest in reading the Bible, but I was not prepared for what I read. My impression of Jesus had been based largely on Hollywood films that portrayed him the way I had always assumed him to be: sincere, kind, always smiling a beatific smile. Then I started reading the Gospels. Here was a man who made the most extraordinary religious claims, yet he threw tables down the front steps of the temple. He asked people how they expected to escape the damnation of hell and said such weak and innocuous things as "I've come to set the earth on fire." I had never had much patience with religious people, and to my great surprise, Jesus had trouble with them too. They accused him of being a drunk and a glutton and having terrible taste in his choice of friends. Here was a man who believed he was the Son of God, and one of the chief complaints against him was that he wasn't religious enough! I liked him immediately!

How I got from this stage of understanding to believing that Jesus was who he said he was began late one evening. I was at a point where I felt desperate to know if God was really there and if the claims of the Bible were true. That night I cried out to God, probably the first prayer I had made in years, that if he was there, I had to know one way or another. If God didn't exist and life was absurd, then I was willing to face that too, but I had to know.

Immediately a thought came to me with penetrating clarity: I should call my childhood minister, Malcolm Nygren. I had gone to Sunday school as a child, but I felt embarrassed to call when I had not seen the pastor in such a long time. But the thought brought me such peace and calm that I was able to sleep.

It took me all the next day to get up my courage, but finally I called. I told him that I was sure he was too busy to see me, but one of these years I might drop in. On the contrary, he said, he would love to see me that day. I gulped and agreed to come after school.

Once in his office, I fired my questions. More than anything else I was hoping that I had misread C. S. Lewis and his interpretation of the Christian faith. I longed for Pastor Nygren to tell me that all that was required to be a Christian was being kind and a good person. He told me what I most dreaded to hear, that I had read Lewis and the biblical faith correctly. Then I said that if being a follower of Jesus meant that we actually come to know him, then it was clear that I was not a Christian, nor had I ever been one. He said I was probably on target. His answers were wise, his manner was sensitive, but he supported the same claims Lewis and the Bible did. I did not feel better, but worse. The weight of the truth of the gospel and its implications left me feeling burdened.

As I was leaving, he told me there was someone he wanted me to meet. Her name was Ethel Renwick. I did meet her and was immediately struck by her remarkable combination of intellect and sensitivity. But there was something else that took me awhile to identify, though I sensed it immediately. She radiated the presence and love of God. It was palpable. I knew she had something that emanated not only from the depth of her being but from the very being of God himself. I wanted what she had.

At the same time I resisted. I have always been amused when people say they wish they could believe as easily as I do. I was hardly a willing convert. I had many unanswered questions. I wanted to live as I had previously—without regard for the existence of God. Yet it seemed as if the minute I finished whatever task was at hand, I would feel a steady, unrelenting presence and pressure, the very one I was seeking to flee. It was odd. I had the sense that God was closing in on me while at the same time I felt I was being offered a free choice.

I knew I was being irresistibly drawn by the sense of a personal God whose love streamed in at every encounter, every sight, every silence. I also knew that the only reasonable response would be a wholehearted commitment. Finally to come to believe that God is God, and then to fail to make him central in one's life, would be folly. It would be like trying to run from the wind.

Although the details of my story are different, the emotions accompanying my own turn to faith are expressed most closely by Lewis:

> I gave in and admitted that God was God and knelt and prayed: Perhaps that night the most dejected and reluctant convert in all England. I did not see

then what is now the most shining and most obvious thing; the Divine humility which will accept a convert even on such terms. The Prodigal Son at least walked home on his two feet. But who can duly adore that Love which will open the high gates to a prodigal who is brought in kicking, struggling, resentful, and darting his eyes in every direction for a chance of escape?[7]

Faith from Beyond Despair

My story is an example of conversion that had most to do with the truth of the message. My search was not motivated by a sense of desperation. My life was not falling apart. Nor did I have a profound sense of my sin. That came later. What prompted my search was a longing to know if God was there and if Jesus' claims were true. What appealed to me was the person of Jesus.

Many other people come to faith out of a great sense of need and desperation. Another friend, whom I'll call Jacob, is an example. I met this remarkable man at a conference I attended for Messianic Jews. These are Jews who believe that Jesus is the Messiah. They do not worship in a Western Christian fashion, but in a manner consistent with their Jewish culture and traditions. As I walked into the courtyard in Haifa where the conference was being held, I saw this man playing with some children. He had a marvelous face, deeply lined and full of character, with eyes that reflected great kindness. Yet what stuck me was how different his face appeared in repose. For when he wasn't engaged in dialogue, deeply etched marks of suffering were painfully apparent.

A few hours later I found myself assigned to a dinner table with him. It was obvious from listening to him that he was a refined, cultured intellectual. He proceeded to tell me his story.

He was an Eastern European Jew. He had prospered professionally, married a Gentile and had one son. Then came World War II and the deportation of the Jews. His Jewish identity was not widely known, and because of his marriage he thought he might be protected from going to prison camp. But one day as he returned home from work, he saw to his horror that the Gestapo were waiting for him. They grabbed him and led him off to the train. His mind was dazed, wondering who had betrayed him. As they were dragging him away, he cried out to one of the soldiers that he hadn't even been allowed to embrace his wife before he left.

The soldier laughed grimly and said, "You fool. Don't you know that it was your wife who tipped us off?"

"You liar!" Jacob cried. "She would never do a thing like that!"

But the soldier replied, "Then you must be the only one who doesn't know. Your wife is having an affair with the chief of police." Jacob looked back at his wife in disbelief and horror. The expression of guilt on her face and her inability to look him in the eyes confirmed that it was true.

He spent the next five years in a prison camp. Several times he nearly died. He certainly hoped that he would. The bitter despair that filled him was the only reminder that he was still alive. One thing, however, occasionally gave him a flicker of hope. If he could survive prison camp, perhaps his son would still be home and they could be reunited. That was the only thought that ever brought light into his darkness.

Finally the war was over and he was released. As he made the long journey home only one thought obsessed him: the intense desire to see his son. When he arrived at his hometown he was told that his wife had left years before to an unknown destination. Somewhere in northern Europe, he was told. She had taken their son with her.

He now knew that he would never see his son again. His last hope was gone. He was physically ill, emaciated, desperately hungry and penniless. He had nowhere to go, so he went to a park bench where the bums of the town gathered.

Even in his misery he could not overlook the irony. These were the men to whom he had given loose change on his way to work in days gone by. Now he was one of them. Before long the police arrested him for loitering. He told the police it was a relief. At least in jail he would get some food and a place to sleep. They saw immediately that he was not a skid row bum but a man in desperate straits. They asked him if he had family. He said he had one brother he had not seen since he was a teenager, who now lived in Tel Aviv. The government decided to pay for the ticket to send him there, as they did not know what else to do with him.

Jacob arrived in Israel with no money. He had hardly eaten in a week and was terribly ill. He went to his brother's home, and the brother would not let him in the door. That is almost unheard of in Jewish culture, but the brother had not seen him in years and refused to believe that the haggard, decrepit-looking bum at his door was really his brother Jacob. He told him to come back with papers to prove that it was really he.

Jacob did not give him the chance to find out. He could not suffer the indignity of one more rejection.

Now he was almost too poor to secure the means to kill himself. And too tired. So he found another park bench where the lowest of the low gathered, and he waited to die. He did not eat, because there was nothing to eat. In his own country he had actually sunk to begging for food, but here he could not bear the humiliation of it. All he thought of was death. He knew it would only be days now.

Several days passed. As he lay on the park bench, at a distance he saw a blond, freshly scrubbed teenage girl, obviously an American, entering the park with a friend. He wondered what on earth someone so innocent and angelic-looking was doing in a park for derelicts. He closed his eyes. Suddenly he heard a soft voice speaking to him. Jacob opened his eyes, and to his astonishment he saw her looking at him with a compassion and sincerity that caught him off guard. It was the first time in six years he had heard anyone speak to him with kindness. He did not know whether to cry in gratitude or laugh in cynicism. But her concern moved him in spite of himself. "What do you want?" he growled at her.

"Sir, I wasn't even supposed to be here in this park. I got off the bus at the wrong place. But when I saw you, and the terrible sadness in your face, I just couldn't leave without telling you something," she said softly.

"Why don't you get back on your bus and leave me alone!" he snapped, appalled as he heard himself sounding as surly as the street people he used to give money to.

"Sir, I was afraid to come over here, but I feel like God is nudging me to tell you something before I get back on my bus. I wish I knew how to say it better, but, well, sir, Jesus loves you. He loves you. He really does."

He looked at her in disbelief. This child was telling him that somebody in heaven loved him? After all the hell he had been though, all the indignity he had suffered, all the rage that had filled his soul for many years, this naive American, who had probably never known a day of real suffering, who had lived a sheltered and protected life, was telling him that some Gentile God loved him. He could not decide whether he was outraged by the audacity or moved that she had taken the effort to talk with him. But as he looked up at her face he saw tears streaming down her cheeks, and to his astonishment he began to weep as well.

"No one could love me, child. It's too late for me," he said between sobs.

"No," she replied urgently as she took his thin, gnarled hand into hers. "It's not too late. God will gladly take you if only you'd let him. Just tell him that you want to. He will love you and help you."

At that moment he knew that Someone was reaching out to him through her. He could not have imagined a more unlikely messenger. But he knew deep within that he was being offered help in his last hour. The choice was his. He decided to take it. He prayed with the American girl on a park bench in the outskirts of nowhere, in his own language. Then he looked at her and said, "I am thankful to you, more than you can ever know. But I am very sick. I am dying."

Then the girl and her friend helped him up, and they took him by bus to the home where they were staying. The family nursed Jacob back to health for one entire year. During the course of that year they shared their faith, read to him from the Bible and prayed with him. Eventually what began as a dying man's desperate invitation to God to take his life became a total commitment of his life and soul to his Messiah.

At the dinner table he laughed and said to the rest of us, "The problem with you Gentiles is that you always keep forgetting that Jesus is Jewish! He belonged to us first!"

Jacob eventually found a good job, moved into his own apartment and went back to his brother and was reconciled. He came to faith in his mid-fifties; when I met him he was in his early seventies. As long as I live I will never forget the expression on his face as he spoke of what the Messiah meant to him. "It would have been so easy," he said, "to have rejected that girl. To have chosen to harbor all the years of resentments and disillusionment in my heart. But to think that God reached out to me, gave me a home and a family who loved me, restored my health and, above all else, filled my heart with a gladness and joy I never knew was possible! You know what I want to do when I get to heaven? I want to be the one who offers a cup of water to everyone else. What could I ever do to express my gratitude to God for all that he has done for me? How will I ever be able to thank God enough? So much has happened in my life since that moment twenty years ago. But the one fact that staggers me most of all is that the girl was right. Jesus loves me. He really does."

The week that I left Israel I tried to get in touch with Jacob to say good-bye. I was told he had suddenly become very sick and the doctors thought he only had days to live. I asked how his spirits were. He was peaceful and serene, they said. There were believers with him at the hospital, and they were reading him psalms and praying and singing hymns.

What a contrast with the bitter, dying man on the park bench a score of years earlier. I asked if he was saying anything. Just one thing, I was told. He was repeating ever so softly: "Jesus loves me."

This extraordinary man and I both came to believe in God through Jesus. Our life experiences could not have been more different. Our objections and fears were poles apart. Yet our two testimonies of God's goodness are identical. As the apostle Peter said to Jesus, "To whom shall we go? You have the words of eternal life" (John 6:68).

Clamence worried that surrendering to God would take away his identity. Having spent more than thirty years in the company of the gospel, I can testify that while God radically transforms us, he leaves us more ourselves than we ever dreamed possible. Clamence worried about his loss of freedom. I marvel at the divine mercy that risks giving us so much.

9

Living the Cross

Christians will have to look more redeemed
if they want me to believe in their redeemer.
FRIEDRICH NIETZSCHE

When a man is getting better, he understands more and more clearly
the evil that is still left in him. When a man is getting worse,
he understands his own badness less and less.
A moderately bad man knows he is not very good;
a thoroughly bad man thinks he is alright.
C. S. LEWIS

One of the most important things to remember when we come to know God is that everything is the same, yet nothing is the same. We still walk the same ground, breathe the same air, drink the same water, buy the same groceries and get buried in the same earth. But like someone falling in love, we find our senses are so heightened that the sky really seems bluer, the grass greener and every second charged with the grandeur of God.

We now know that each step we take is an accompanied step, and far beyond the steps we see, our lives are reordered by a new and blazing vision that moves ahead. The journey home may be long and hard, but at the end is home, and the One who waits for us is Father. To live the Chris-

tian life well is to know what the very purpose of life is. In the famous
words of the Westminster Shorter Catechism: "What is the chief end of
man? To glorify God and enjoy him forever."

How can we do otherwise once we see who God is? And how can we fail
to seize the reality of purpose when we hear God say, "I have a future for
you, of hope and not despair"? Or when we realize the lengths to which he
has gone already to support us in the trials of life?

> Fear not, for I have redeemed you;
>> I have called you by name; you are mine.
> When you pass through the waters,
>> I will be with you;
> and when you pass through the rivers,
>> they will not sweep over you.
> When you walk through the fire,
>> you will not be burned;
>> the flames will not set you ablaze. . . .
> You are precious and honored in my sight. (Isaiah 43:1-4)

Only when we taste and see that the Lord is good, as the psalmist tells
us, do we gain the right motive and framework from which to live our lives.
Difficulties and suffering will come. There will be trials to overcome, pain
to endure, temptations to conquer, but the thrust of our lives is ordered by
one thing: a response with the totality of our being to his love and living a
life worthy of that love.

The School of the Cross

What enabled us to confront ourselves and look at our condition in the first
place was the cross. But the lessons of the cross are ones we never outgrow,
for the further we go the deeper we get.

What does this mean? It means, first, that we are taught to live humbly.
The cross forever mirrors to us our sin, so we live before God in meekness,
not self-righteousness. Once we were proud, carelessly thinking too much
of ourselves, although the religion of self-righteousness is as far from God
as it is possible to get. Now we know that we have nothing we have not
been given, so all that we do comes from a heart cleared of presumption

and at peace with reality. What an empty folly is conceit after that.

Next, the cross teaches us to live gratefully. The Christian life is a thank-you from beginning to end as we ponder what God has done. What an absurdity to think that we could ever bargain with God, as if there were anything we could put on the table. Nothing we can do would ever earn his favor. Yet all is ours for free. And the cross reveals his willingness to forgive not just once but over and over and over again. How can we repay such extravagant, generous love? We cannot and need not, and the heart's only answer is gratitude.

The street woman who gate-crashes Simon's banquet to see Jesus shows us how to approach God with an unrestrained heart of gratitude (see Luke 7:36-50). She is clearly a sensual woman. She has spent her life in bed with men, adored and appreciated by many while scorned and rejected by others. But as she approaches Christ, it is clear that something earthshaking has taken place within her, making her feel that her life has been turned upside down. She can no longer hold it back. She begins to sob, and as her tears rain down on his feet, she lets down her hair and dries them with it.

In the shocked stillness of the room, it is clear to everyone that she has offered her all. Called into question himself, Simon calls on Jesus to stop this bare-souled act. But no. Jesus receives her gift—in her way, in her style. He knows that this act of intimacy, of being touched by a woman—especially one of ill repute—will make him further outcast in the eyes of the respectable. But Jesus is determined to let this stand. All that matters is the thanks wrung from the depth of the woman's being.

Her great love, Jesus sums up, shows how much she has been forgiven. So the New Testament's premier example of gratitude and faith is a forgiven prostitute.

Saying No to Self

Humility and gratitude sometimes appear quiet and easily assumed virtues. Doubtless the inside stories would be different if we knew them, but the school of the cross teaches hard, unsentimental truths as well. One of them is that we are called to say no—a radical, total, final, unconditional no—to the self that is the center of our egotism. Only as we cut off sin stone dead can we know new life in the Spirit. Only as we literally "put to death" the old nature (Matthew 5:30) can we walk in the power of God.

Our problem, of course, is that we want to gain the blessings without the pain. We want to add on without taking anything away. But the Bible is clear about what we are to die to and to live for. Things such as envy, slander, malice, jealousy, anger, selfishness, impurity and idolatry are to be put away. Love, joy, peace, patience, kindness, goodness, faithfulness, gentleness and self-control are to be put on in their place.

Remember, God wants us to confess and cease from sin so we can be free of it and enjoy the greatest freedom of all—joy. His desire is that we live in the light, which is why he prods us to face our darkness. A recurring theme here, and a relentlessly recurring theme in the Bible, is that to experience the miracle of God's grace we must continually face the mess within. One leads to the other. Knowing that God is our Creator and that he is good, we would be choosing insanity, not to mention defeating ourselves, not to do as he instructs.

Thus whenever our life is in conflict with God's truth as revealed in the Bible, we must change. When the self contradicts the will of God, we deny the self. When the self chooses sin, we say no to it. When the self wants to put our interests above the interests of others, we side with love against the self. There are times we sacrifice our desires for the other's sake. Surely any parent knows this lesson firsthand. To live the way of the cross means we say yes to God and no to self. But we will eventually be amazed at the new self that emerges as a result.

The pattern for living the way of the cross can be seen in the one who went to the cross: "My Father, . . . not as I will, but as you will" (Matthew 26:39). His followers, Jesus said bluntly, are to follow him: "If anyone would come after me, he must deny himself and take up his cross and follow me" (Matthew 16:24).

But wait a minute, someone will say. This call to deny the self is surely the very denial we have been seeking to put a stop to. When we deny ourselves at a certain point, aren't we losing touch with our own humanity? If we do not do what we want to do, are we really free? And worse still, are we psychologically healthy?

That's a natural response, but to deny the self is not the same as denial.

To say no to self does not mean we are not listening to our desires. To deny self, when self is in conflict with God, is to save and protect our humanity. What we are saying no to is the lie, the deception, the flaw, that left unchecked would destroy our humanity. Far from deceiving ourselves by denying self when self wants to sin, we are at last seeing clearly. When it contradicts the will of God, it's self that is deceived. God always wills our best. Again, the analogy of the human parent and child works perfectly. There are many instincts, desires and natural gifts in our children that we want to nurture and foster. Other instincts and desires must be disciplined, restrained and redirected or they will literally ruin the child's life.

But make no mistake, the biblical call to self-denial will sound like a strange tune to the modern ear, for all we hear today is that the key to everything is self-love. Find yourself. Be true to yourself. Feel good about yourself. Even advertising campaigns for national charities have found that the lucrative appeal is to give so you can feel good about yourself. Self-indulgence is your right. The indispensable element of modern growth, our culture seems to say, is maturity in self-love. Endlessly and from all sides, the wisdom of our age is that we must love ourselves. It is above all else now the American way.

A Hate I Hated to Admit

Let me tell you of an experience that taught me the tough lesson of saying no to self. A woman I know (whom I'll call Amy) has caused a great deal of pain to some very close friends of mine. Several years ago I said to a friend, Liz, "I finally realized something—I hate Amy." For me to be able to admit that was a big step. Being a "people person" by nature and a Christian besides, I was devastated to acknowledge that kind of poison inside me.

To my utter astonishment, Liz said, "Yes, Becky, I have known that a long time. But I felt it was something you had to see on your own."

I felt overwhelmed. I said, "I don't have the slightest idea where to go with this hate. I know that God is the only one who can change my heart, but what is my responsibility? Jesus says we are to love our enemies. I could no more love Amy than fly. So what am I supposed to do now?"

Liz answered, "Well, first, quit gossiping about her. Every time you get together with the others, you all talk about Amy and dredge up what she did. My suggestion is to quit gossiping. Just stop talking about her."

With a flicker of irritation I said, "Well, who asked your opinion?"

"You did!"

Now what was the big deal about gossiping? It felt like such a little thing in light of all that this person had done to people I care about. Yet where did it lead me? Did it lead me to joy and freedom? Hardly. It simply caused me to spiral down into the pit of bitterness and a desire for vengeance.

I clearly saw that although I could not make my heart loving toward Amy, I *could* stop gossiping. So I quit talking about her in a negative way. It is almost embarrassing to admit how much it helped. For one thing I was not dredging up all of that pain continually.

Then a new challenge emerged. I would be going along fine when suddenly a thought about Amy would come. All of the old poison would rise up in me. Finally, one day I asked God for help. The next day I read a verse in the Bible from Paul's second letter to Corinth: "We take captive every thought to make it obedient to Christ" (2 Corinthians 10:5). As I pondered the meaning of that in light of my problem, a new idea came to me. It sounds painfully obvious, but it had not occurred to me that it was my choice whether I chose to feed on hateful thoughts. For each time a fiery dart was launched in my mind, I had always followed it along and eventually retraced the slow spiral descent to which it led. After that I prayed that I would become aware of the first intrusion of a critical thought. It would be far easier to expel such thoughts at that stage than later.

That same day I was listening to the radio and heard a psychologist discuss what she called "stop thoughts." Her point was that if we do not want to entertain destructive thoughts, we have the option of not doing so. She suggested that after refusing them entry into our minds, we should get up and immediately do something physical and active.

Then I realized that I had not distinguished between temptation and sin. I was being tempted to the sin of hatred by these thoughts, but I did not have to succumb. So when the thoughts popped into my mind, I turned to the Lord and said, "I do not want to hate, but I cannot love. Please give me the strength not to indulge in these thoughts, for they only make me miserable and separated from you. From now on, with your help I am choosing not to allow them into my heart."

God did help me, yet it was clear how important my own obedience was. I took several other steps in the process, and only in retrospect did I see that each tiny step was preparing me for the biggest step of all: to pray for Amy.

One day God seemed to say to me: "Becky, you have never prayed for her. Why don't you?"

"No way," I said to God. Because I knew that if I prayed for her, I would start to care about her. And that was the last thing I wanted to happen. Amy had done great wrongs, and I did not want God to try to change my mind.

But John Calvin was right. Grace is irresistible. My hard heart was no match for God's love. I gave in and prayed for her. And the moment I simply said her name, I started to cry. I found myself asking questions: What was her story? What kind of background did she come from? What had shaped her such that she could be so full of venom? And then I prayed for myself. What blinders was I wearing that prevented my seeing any good in Amy?

Slowly, in this way, my heart began to soften. I can't remember when it was precisely, but one day it dawned on me that the poison of hatred was gone. Amy did not become an intimate friend. Jesus, after all, told us to love our *enemy*. He did not promise that loving an enemy would suddenly turn them into best buddies. But I can honestly say that as I obeyed what God showed me, he changed my heart of stone to a heart of flesh.

In my enthusiasm over what God was doing in my life, I began to press others to look deeply at their sin. That was a mistake. We should share the good things that God is doing in our lives. But our tendency is to want others to grasp in five minutes what it took us five years to understand. Our growth from self-concealment to self-revelation needs to pace with God's timing, since God knows us perfectly and knows what we are able to bear. To insist that a young convert, or a teen from a devout home, have a penetrating understanding of sin is not our business. Young converts may not be psychologically or spiritually ready for that. We leave that to God. He will assure that one day it happens. That is what the journey is all about: from

seeing ourselves for who we really are to surrendering ourselves totally to
God so he can change us.

It's Tough and It Takes Time

I learned a lot from that experience. I learned that freedom came through
denying self and tackling hate, rather than indulging in the feelings. I
learned that we must not let our spirits flag in the battle with sin. To see the
victory of God's grace over sin is not something we can knock off in a weekend. Though we live in a culture that is always in a hurry and demands
instant results, the Bible admonishes us to wait, to work at it and never to
lose heart.

I have discovered no magic key that enables us to lock out suffering or
fast-forward through the painful and often slow process of growth. I have
found no shortcuts, no gimmicks to becoming the person God desires. Evil
never has the last word, God does. But while we wait, we need to ask for
the grace of tenacity, so that we can hang on—and on—and on while he
works his excellent purpose in us.

I learned, too, that while God convicted me of sin, he never condemned
me. My inner feelings of self-condemnation during my slow progress and
even my sense of failure were never from God. We can lose our perspective
while we are dealing with what is wrong with us. So we need to remember
that it is not God's desire that we live in perpetual pain, morbidly focused
on what is wrong. That tactic is the Enemy's, not God's. God convicts us of
sin only so we may be forgiven and enabled to walk in freedom.

Since that time, I have been deeply sobered by the thought of what
would have happened if I had allowed the hate to grow. Confession is not a
list of petty blemishes drawn up grudgingly to satisfy an overbearing God.
It is a facing up to those cancerous vices that sap vitality, cripple freedom
and eventually kill. We are the ones who suffer if we sin. Conversely, God
radically opposes sin, but only because he loves us.

Was it cruel of God to ask me to deal with the poison of my hate and
learn to love my enemy? If I were out camping and were bitten by a snake,
the immediate thing to do would be to use a razor and cut open the wound
and let out the venom. Using the razor would not be cruel; it would be sav-

ing my life! So it is with God. But the fact that God wills our best does not mean we will like it.

> It is true there is difficulty in entering into godliness. But this difficulty does not arise from the religion which begins in us, but only from the irreligion which is still there. If our senses were not opposed to penitence, and if our corruption were not opposed to the purity of God, there would be nothing in this painful to us. We suffer only in proportion as the vice which is natural to us resists supernatural grace. Our heart feels torn asunder between these opposed efforts. But it would be very unfair to impute this violence to God, who is drawing us on, instead of to the world, which is holding us back. . . . The cruelest war that God can make with men in this life is to leave them without that war which He came to bring. "I came to bring fire and the sword." Before Him the world lived in this false peace.[1]

The requirement of toughness means we must approach life as if we were soldiers, not weekend golfers. Some people expect that life will be no more demanding or complicated than riding a golf cart over Astroturf. When battles come they are unprepared. Would it not be wiser and more realistic to think of and experience life as on a soldier's Jeep? We may have a bumpy ride, but we will learn the terrain of sin and grace firsthand, finding out the pitfalls to be avoided and where the resources are to be found.

God will use the difficulties and trials of our lives to make us strong. The apostle James tells us to greet our trials as friends and let them be teachers molding our character (James 1:2-4). We must be ruthless in not allowing sin to make its home in us. The "friend" is not the sin but the potential avenue of growth in godliness that it brings.

Aligning our will with God's is not something that happens automatically or overnight. There will be a battle as we seek to surrender our lives to the will of God. We shouldn't underestimate the pain that will be involved. But neither must we forget what is happening to us: We are being changed into the likeness of God.

Since we moderns assume that the purpose of life is not to be good but to feel good, the struggle of meshing our will with God's becomes an even greater challenge. Ancients believed that life's purpose was in the attainment of character and virtue. But our modern lens has been altered. We speak of progress but have no purpose. We value drive but have no direction. In his book *Making Sense out of Suffering*[2] Peter Kreeft observes that a problem of the "feel-good" approach to life is that we become incapable of coping with suffering. We try to back out the minute the going gets tough because suffering, by definition within the feel-good framework, does not make anyone feel good. Therefore we moderns think suffering must be avoided at any cost. But when we know the purpose and realize that God is in the process of making us godly, of shaping us to be like him, the pain seems less important than the outcome. As Paul wrote to the Christians in Corinth, "For our light and momentary troubles are achieving for us an eternal glory that far outweighs them all" (2 Corinthians 4:17).

Power and Will

What resources have we been given to help us conquer sin? First, we have the power made available in the cross itself. The first lesson of the cross is that we must never underestimate evil—we crucified Christ. The second lesson is that we must not overestimate evil either. As we trust in Christ, we are identified with him, so that *in him* it is as if we were crucified too.

The cross does more than show us that God longs for us to be free from what destroys us. It does more than reveal the price paid for our deliverance. At its heart is the most potent energy in the universe that breaks the grip of evil, cancels its tight hold over us and rolls back the tyranny of its control. Once we accept what Christ has done for us on the cross, for the first time we have a real choice not to sin. Before then we were entirely predictable. For all our cheery press releases about "choice," "autonomy" and "authenticity," anyone at all could figure out the way we would behave by calculating what was really in our self-interest. When push came to shove, that was the consideration that counted. Self-centeredness was such a habit that we could no more kick it than any other addiction. But Christ died so that the power of our self-centeredness could be broken. The power of evil was broken so we can live new lives. If we belong to God, we benefit from what he accomplished on the cross.

So we are helpless by ourselves, and only God has the power. Perhaps we then sit back and watch? No, says the Bible: if the power is God's, the responsibility to work out what he has worked in is ours. Our part is to be willing, in the sense of exercising the will, to put to death whatever gets in the way of our becoming the person God desires. The Bible minces no words on the subject. Jesus tells us that when we see things in our lives that should not be there, we are to be ruthless. Pluck it out, cut it off, get completely rid of it. The graphic language emphasizes that the contest is brutal and our wills crucial in the severe treatment sin requires.

The story of the paralytic man in the Gospel of John is a telling example (John 5:1-9). Unable to get to the Pool of Bethesda waters only a few feet away so that he might be healed, he complains to Jesus that no one would take him. He has sat there, paralyzed and complaining, for thirty years! But Jesus sidesteps the obvious plea for help and asks him first, "Do you want to get well?"

Jesus is not hoodwinked by the man's underlying suggestion that he would have been walking by now, but nothing has worked and no one will help. Jesus is willing and able to help, but only if the man is willing to exercise his will and do as Jesus says: "Get up! Pick up your mat and walk."

Christ's part is to break the power of evil; ours is to submit our will to him. A new way of living has been opened up as a result of Christ's death, because the backbone of our rebellion has been broken. We have been moved from the enemy camp, where we had no choice, to God's camp, where we do. Now the critical choice—to choose not to sin—can be made, and it is ours to make.

New Nature, New Habits

Our first steps away from sin and our first steps in the Spirit begin with a deliberate change of habits. Habits are a form of trained "second nature," and our new nature requires new habits. Only God can change our hearts, but we can change our behavior.

Yet make no mistake. If our recovery from sin is to be complete, far more is needed than a change in behavior and the forming of new habits. We need the power of God to change our hearts.

But that power works in two directions at once: it deals with the heart from the inside out and with the habits from the outside in. And both as we obey. Martin Luther King Jr. once observed that although he could not make other people love him, he could so live as to compel them to treat him properly. Similarly, changed habits can be a step toward changed hearts, because the seriousness it takes to change a habit is a sign of the seriousness of the faith required to have the heart changed.

Some Christians say that no struggling and wrestling are required in the Christian life. All we must do is "let go and let God." They are right that God alone can change our hearts. But the biblical writers make no bones about the part we have to play, which suggests that in our growth, our habits are nearly as important as our hearts. Perhaps not least because they mirror the heart. So we must embrace both truths: God is at work in us to transform our hearts and make us into his image, while our wills must work on resolutely to train our habits to conform to his will.

The Crash of Falling Idols

Training new habits can be spectacular in hindsight, particularly under the magnifying-glass conditions of a public testimony. But the day-to-day work, of course, is rather more dogged than sensational. Not so with the next part of the school of the cross—pulling down idols, or false gods.

As soon as we come to know God, we confront an immediate, unconditional and permanent requirement of discipleship: "You shall have no other gods before me" (Exodus 20:3). What is an idol? Anyone or anything we are committed to absolutely apart from God, or trusting in for our security other than God. Is there something we desperately want? Anything we feel we must have or life will lose its meaning? A person or object who represents for us a desire on which we would build our life instead of on God? That is what the Bible calls an idol.

Do you remember how often we've seen that "playing God" is at the unmasked heart of sin? So at bottom our idols are a lie, a fraudulent fiction, but utterly invaluable as a strategy to help us to stay in control. What we are worshiping or leaning on for security may not be bad in itself. But next to God, the created up against the uncreated, the finest and worthiest of finite things are false and painted shams. The good becomes the deadly enemy of the best.

Many of us fashion idols out of our desire for power, approval, comfort and control. And once erected, each has its own lies and fears. The lie associated with the idol of power is that unless we are winning and on top, life has no meaning. The fear that accompanies it is the fear of losing. The lie of the idol of approval is that life has meaning only if a certain person or people like us; the corresponding fear is of rejection. The lie of the idol of comfort and security is that we must have a life that is secure and without pain or we will never find contentment; the fear is of suffering of any kind. The lie of the idol of control is that unless we are in charge and seeing to it that everyone around us is living up to our standards, then life can never be satisfying; the fear is the fear of failure.

Newly converted believers sometimes imagine they've been more successful at toppling idols than they have. Deities, even false ones, are not so easily dislodged. After all, we're so used to them that we have grown like them—we've become what we worship (see Psalm 115:4-8). So while it's easy to lop off the outward manifestation of sin, the root trails underground. When it sprouts again, it will probably be disguised in a subtle form that makes it hard to detect.

For example, let's say we were extremely competitive and had an appetite for power before we embraced faith. For a while we have a honeymoon period when it all feels easy. But as things settle down, what we slowly come to see is that our lust for power is slipping back in a religious guise: We have to be the leader, we have to dominate the church discussion group, our worth is in the numbers of other people we have led to faith, and so forth. So while we say our confidence is solely in Christ, the truth is that we are still depending on the old props, operating through the same false idols we used to exploit.

A nun once told me that after she took the vow of poverty she said to herself, *I am no longer acquisitive and competitive like the rest of the world.* But as the years passed, she realized she was keenly concerned over whether she got the religious duties, the pupils and the favored appointments she longed for. "Finally," she said, "I had to face the fact that I was very acquisitive. I was just competing for different things than I had in my previous secular life. My acquisitive nature was still there, only in disguised forms.

The breakthrough came when I faced myself and acknowledged to God the sin I had been denying: I was a highly competitive, acquisitive person. Though it was painful to admit, it was when I confessed it as sin that God began to change me."

Good Morning, Fellow Sinners!

One of the idols that must hit the dust is our old lust for feigned innocence. Living the cross requires us to give up pretending there is nothing wrong with us. As strong as the old tendency is toward denial and always putting ourselves in the best possible light, the cross cuts through our façade. No matter how innocently we smile or how much energy we expend on image control, it's all a waste of time. The cross will always be confronting us, the central reality of history before which no fiction can endure.

One practical benefit is that the cross frees us to communicate with one another in a spirit of openness and honesty, without pretense. That does not mean we bare our souls every time we hear a casual "How are you?" But it means we can strive for conversation that has integrity.

In 1979 Bishop Fulton Sheen addressed the annual National Prayer Breakfast in Washington—a group of national and international leaders, with official Washington heavily represented. "Fellow sinners!" he greeted the elite crowd. It was amusing to see so many people squirming all at once. "We Americans do not like to hear about sin. We Catholics believe in the Immaculate Conception of the Blessed Virgin Mary. . . . Now all Americans believe that they are immaculately conceived. There is no sin, we just make mistakes."[3]

Bishop Sheen hit the nail on the head. There's a terrible trap in modern notions of "total transparency" in relationships, but the main problem we will face as we seek to live in openness is that we encounter people still vigorously denying the truth about themselves. But that does not mean that we need to live that way. Though again, a caution. We must be wise about whom we trust and at what level we open up. What I am arguing for is an attitude of openness and refreshing candor about ourselves, as opposed to pretense and image control. It goes without saying that openness should not be translated as "letting it all hang out," a rather more peculiarly American phenomenon.

I remember taking part in a small group that was studying the Bible. There was a delightful woman in the group, someone who taught me a great deal about living for God. However, she was of the school, though she may not have realized it, that it is a sin to admit one is a sinner. She would, of course, say she believed in the doctrine of sin, but she never spoke of anything but "victory."

One day the leader of the study asked us, "What do you think controls you that shouldn't?"

We knew one another well by then, so there was enough trust to be able to speak openly. The "victorious" woman spoke up at once. "The besetting sin of my life," she said, "is that I just don't write as many letters as I should."

There was a long silence. Not surprisingly, no one "shared" after that! The lid on the discussion had been clamped shut.

Mind you, I said she was a delightful woman. Yet I wanted to ask her (though I didn't), "Is that why Christ died? Because we did not write enough letters? That seems like a stiff price to pay just because we lacked enough stamps."

No Longer Lone Rangers

I heard a famous Christian say on television, "People ask me if I have any problems with my children or ever have tiffs with my wife. And I say maybe I do and maybe I don't, but I'm not going to tell you about it. I just go to God!" He continued, "Oh people, don't tell one another about your petty little problems. You must be a winner, a champion, a success for the Lord!" Then he quoted from a poem that he said summed up the Christian life. I did not take notes, but it went something like this: "Feel down? Feel discouraged? Be a man! Feel like throwing in the towel? Be a man! Feel like sharing your burdens? Be a man! Feel like giving up? Be a man! Be a man! Be a man!"

It would be safe to say that this would not qualify as one of my favorite poems! First, I find it difficult to identify with the refrain. But the larger problem was the speaker's perception that even acknowledging a problem or temptation dishonors God. Wouldn't it be refreshing to hear over the television airwaves what the apostle Paul claimed: "I am the chief of sinners" (see 1 Timothy 1:15-16)? When Paul talked about his "thorn in the flesh," I do not recall Jesus saying to him, "Oh, Paul, for crying out loud! Just buck up and be a man! It's so embarrassing how you share this with everybody. And have you ever stopped to consider how it makes me look?" No, that is not what Jesus said. Rather, he told Paul, "I will not take this thorn away from you, because I am glorified in your weakness" (see 2 Corinthians 12:7-9).

The man on television had done what most of us do without realizing it. He took a secular, popular Americana myth and simply spiritualized it. He took the Lone Ranger cowboy image and added some god-talk. What he was really saying was "All I need in life is God and my horse, and we'll ride out into the sunset together. If I've got a problem, I'll tell my horse." But that is the gospel according to Louis L'Amour. Many Christians are aware of cults, but they miss ones like this. This is the American "cowboy cult," the appeal of the "Marlboro man" transferred to the Christian faith.

The cross makes this kind of image control under the guise of spirituality seem ludicrous. The cross is all about power, but an upside-down power seen more clearly in our weakness than in strength.

When Cross-Eyed Is Clear-Sighted

Dust, rusty nails and blood notwithstanding, the ground at the foot of the cross is the only vantage point from which to view life clearly. To see things there is to see them truly.

Take racism. The cross makes racism repugnant. If all of us are sinners, how can we ever justify an attitude of racial superiority? Living in Jerusalem for three years made me deeply aware of the racism in anti-Semitism and anti-Arabism. Surely there is something singularly evil about using the cross as a tool against Jews throughout history. We have used the one reality that exposes all of us as guilty to justify the evil of our charge against some: "The Jews killed Christ." As far as I know, anti-Semitism and the teachings of related groups such as the Ku Klux Klan are the only forms of collective evil that compound their evils by perpetrating them in conscious reference to our most precious symbol—the cross.

At a far more ordinary level, the cross frees us to relate to all kinds of people, whether they share our faith or not. Some Christians avoid relationships with people who are not Christians, and the reasons they give are baffling. "They are sinners!" I've heard people say. So? Aren't we all? Is sin that foreign to us? Friendship does not mean that we compromise our beliefs. We are called by God to identify, not to be identical. We are free to embrace others warmly no matter how different they may seem. Christ had to go to the cross for *our* sins just as much as he did for theirs.

When I met Helen, she was not a believer. She has always been larger than life in temperament, very bright and, as I came to discover, extremely sensitive. Helen had almost no church background and was intrigued that I took my faith seriously but was not interested for herself. Her husband, Mel, was so surprised that she had befriended someone "religious" that he asked her to arrange a lunch so he could meet me. During the course of the meal Mel said, "I know that you are very religious. To be perfectly honest, we aren't. We try to have an open relationship—you know, a modern marriage." He hadn't made fully clear what he meant, but I had a sneaking suspicion that the idea was not as modern as he thought! Sure enough, he said, "We both have affairs, and we acknowledge it openly. It's just no big deal."

As our friendship grew, I discovered that his description was not really true of his wife. Unbeknownest to him, Helen was not involved with lots of men. Rather she was desperately involved with one. And she was tormented because she wanted to be with him greatly, but not at the expense of leaving her children. I listened for hours as she tried to work out what she would do and to make sense out of her situation. All the while, I shared my own faith when I felt it was appropriate, and I strongly encouraged her to begin reading the Bible. But she always told me she was sure she would not understand a page of it, as she was not religious.

One day Helen came over to my home and said, "I have some specific questions for you on the Gospel of Mark." I was elated, because I assumed it was the result of all my prayers for her and my constant encouragement for her to read the Bible. I quickly learned otherwise.

"I was with my lover the other day," she said, "and out of the blue he asked me what I thought about Jesus. I thought I wasn't hearing him correctly, so I asked him to repeat it. Then he said, 'I've never read the New Testament, so I decided that as a thinking person I should at least know what it says. I have a lot of questions, but what I wasn't prepared for was the appeal of Jesus. I was thunderstruck by him. I've begun asking my friends if they knew much about Jesus and what their conclusions were. But they haven't been much help. So I thought maybe you knew something and could help me.'"

I was amused when she told me what her response to her lover was: "I told him that I take all my religious questions to Becky, and that he should write them out on a piece of paper and I would get back to him." Then she added casually, "He told me that the next time we get together, among other things, he wants to have a Bible study on the Gospel of Mark."

I have heard of some unlikely settings for a Bible study, but this one would definitely take first prize! It moved me to contemplate the kind of God this story revealed. Where would most people expect to find God? In a church or someplace respectable, surely. And where did my friend first begin to search for God? In a place where people should not be: violating their marriage vows, potentially hurting their children, breaking faith with their spouses. Yet God was right there in their midst, seeking to draw their attention, loving them, calling them. He is not dissuaded by our blindness and lostness. He seeks us where we are. He does not wait until our lives are in order before he will have anything to do with us.

"There is one thing that I want you to do," I said. "If you are going to have a Bible study anyway, have one with me first and you can study the same passage with him afterward." So we began meeting at her home for Bible studies.

The first time I could tell that Helen was nervous. Within a few minutes she leaned over the Bible and said in a hushed whisper, "Can I ask you something? Do you think the Bible would object if I smoked a little cigarillo? I mean, can you do that in front of the Bible?"

I laughed and told her that of course it was all right. I had the feeling that she half-expected the Bible to answer her back in a scolding baritone voice.

A little while later she leaned over the Bible and again asked in a hushed voice, "Do you think I could have just a little glass of wine?" I told her that she was in her home and I wanted her to feel as comfortable as possible.

From then on we got together weekly, she with a cigarillo in one hand, a glass of wine in the other, as we looked at who Jesus was. Then she would take what we had studied and share it with her lover a few days later.

One time was especially memorable. We had been studying the passage where Jesus meets the prostitute at Simon's banquet. She looked straight at me and said, "I just can't get over Jesus. He is so opposite of everything I had imagined him to be. All my life I have felt like I was worth a piece of dirt. And if there is a God, I was sure that he went along with my opinion. But he doesn't. No one has to tell me I am lost. I know I'm lost. If there's a God, I assumed he despised my lostness. But as we've been reading the Bible it seems that Jesus doesn't despise you if you're lost; in fact he loves you if you're lost. And according to Jesus, if you're lost and you *know* that you are lost, you are probably close to the kingdom of God. Can you imagine that—someone like me close to the kingdom of God?"

"Oh yes, I can," I said to her. "I can imagine it very easily." Tears welled up in my eyes as I tried to explain: "You see, I can't get over Jesus either. He is all that you are seeing and even more. I've been a Christian now for many years, and the obedience is not easier, but the joy is so much deeper. You may never decide to give your life to God, which would be tragic. But now that you have caught a glimpse of what Jesus is truly like, I don't think you will ever be quite the same."

After that particular Bible study there were significant changes. She broke off the relationship with the other man. A few weeks later her husband, Mel, was offered a new job, which meant their entire family had to move to another country. She called me after they arrived and said, "You won't believe this, but I've started going to church. I met this minister and his wife, and I don't know quite how to explain it, but they remind me of you! Oh Becky, if only I could believe there could be a God who personally cares for me."

I love Helen. I count it a privilege to be her friend. And I understand how hard it has been for her to believe that there is an invisible God in heaven who loves her when her human experience of love has been so unsatisfactory.

How can I have the freedom to love Helen so deeply? Made in the image of God, we share a common humanity. But deeper still, the cross shows me that I am no different from her. Do you think it matters to Jesus that my list of sins is not the same as hers? That seems pretty irrelevant. Mine cost Jesus his life just as hers did. That is why we can all reach out to those around us with outstretched arms. We do so out of sheer gratitude for what God has done for us—and because we know that if he can change us, he can change anybody. In one way, the cross divides. It draws a line across history. It stands between good and evil, truth and lies. But in another way, it unites. The cross is the leveling ground on which differences of status, success and character are swallowed up before a judgment and a mercy that exclude no one.

The cross also stands as a reminder that God has his own timetable and we must be patient. There was a long period of waiting from the story of Adam and Eve's fall until the coming of Christ. God had to prepare the way to get things in order for the coming of Christ. So will it be with our seeking friends.

The story about Helen happened over fourteen years ago. Over those years she experienced some great difficulties that caused her to give up her search for God. I was grieved to hear that she had turned her back on faith. Nevertheless I prayed.

Then from out of the blue I received an e-mail last year from her. After catching me up on her past she concluded: "But this you must know—thanks to endless discussions with my son, my indebtedness to your original witness and the ever-patient love and consistent example of our dear mutual friend—I have at last finally succumbed to his grace. I was lost but now I'm found; was blind but now I see."

The Bible tells us that "the Lord . . . is patient with you, not wanting anyone to perish, but everyone to come to repentance" (2 Peter 3:9). Helen's conversion reminded me once again that all is grace—whether it takes fourteen years or forty.

10

Living
the Resurrection

The kingdom of God is not a matter of talk but of power.

May you know what is the hope of your calling, . . . and how vast are the resources
of his power, open to those who trust in him, measured by the might he exerted in
Christ when he raised him from the dead.
PAUL OF TARSUS

In his great classic *The City of God* Augustine describes our condition on
earth as a form of citizenship in two cities, the city of man and the City of
God. The lure of the city of man often silences the summons of the call of
the City of God. Earth's city is visible, solid, apparent to our senses and
always alluring. God's city, by contrast, appears hidden, uncertain and very
far away. But appearances are deceptive, for the City of God is the real, the
substantial and the lasting, while the city of man proves fleeting and vain.

Next to the immediacy of the city of man, which promises to meet our
needs right now, God's promise does not seem like much. But when all the
broken promises of the city of man are strewn like cast-off baubles in the
ash heaps of life, it means everything to know that we can know God, and

in knowing him find what our hearts long for.

We are not to renounce our citizenship in the city of man, but as we strengthen our citizenship in the City of God, we find a fulfillment more satisfying than any the other could have offered. We must be patient, for it takes time to build our citizenship in the City of God. But our purpose in this chapter is to understand how the resurrection both opens the way from one city to another and shapes our lives as we live with our dual citizenship.

Above all, the resurrection tells us that we are spiritual beings whose true nature is discovered and fulfilled only as we live in intimacy with God. We have seen the central truth of living the cross: whenever our thoughts, words or deeds are at odds with the will of God, we must deny ourselves and put to death every trace of sin in our lives. And not just once, but over and over again. Here we look at living the resurrection: how a way has been opened up enabling us to meet God and receive all he has for us—his power, nature, help and gifts.

The cross prompts us to serve God in a spirit of humility because it reveals our sin. The resurrection, by revealing the power of God to bring life to the powerless, moves us to relinquish control and depend on the only real source of power—the Holy Spirit. The cross, by revealing the offer of God's forgiveness through Christ, moves us to a life lived in gratitude. The resurrection, by revealing the rich provision of God's grace through Christ, moves us to respond in faith and joy.

The Living God

The resurrection shows us that God is alive. He is really there. He speaks and out of nothing calls reality into being. His mighty acts in history are unquestionable. Thus in the Bible he is often called "the living God." The ancient Hebrews who used this term were not interested merely in whether God existed, as if he were simply a Prime Mover or the last step in a philosopher's syllogism. What mattered to them was that he is alive and personal. He is involved in the affairs of this planet. His presence makes a real difference.

In the Bible, *living* means vibrant and dynamic. To speak of God as "the living God" is to make the claim that God is actively present, here and now.

He is a person who has qualities: He loves, hates, pities, has compassion. We in turn can ignore him, hate him, argue with him, reject him, know him, but only because he is alive!

If God is described in the Bible as "the living God," then it is no surprise that wherever he is present and whatever he creates also shows this vital dynamism. For example, the letter to the Hebrews states: "The Word of God is living and active. Sharper than any double-edged sword, it penetrates even to dividing soul and spirit, joints and marrow; it judges the thoughts and attitudes of the heart" (Hebrews 4:12). The apostle Paul writes that when we worship God, "we, who with unveiled faces all reflect the Lord's glory, are being transformed into his likeness with ever-increasing glory, which comes from the Lord, who is the Spirit" (2 Corinthians 3:18). James, the brother of Jesus, writes that when Christians pray together, they should remember to "confess your sins to each other and pray for each other so that you may be healed" (James 5:16). In each case there is a strong sense of changing power, and it is clear that God's Spirit uses these active agents of grace to transform utterly those who use them.

What enables us to live this new life, and to benefit from these means of grace, is the power unleashed by Christ's rising from the dead. He did more than die and pay the penalty of sin. He was raised from death itself, and the very power God used to raise him is the power made available to us. Through the resurrection God now offers us new life. Eternal life is the life of eternity brought forward to start in time. Living the resurrection is living in the old world by the energy of the new world to come.

Securing the Still Center

Knowing God does not just happen in an instant. To know God requires not just ecstasy and experience but work, study, reflection and prayer. In the middle of crazy lives, we need to secure a still center. We will be busy in enterprises of one sort or another and will have need to be with fellow Christians, but we must also take time to be quiet, to create space in our day to read the Bible and to pray, to slow down enough so we can think, listen and meditate quietly, without demanding or rushing.

This is not easy to do if you are living at the beginning of the twenty-first century! Modernity works against knowing God. We are encouraged to run, not reflect; to do three things at once, not one thing well. We prize the ability to drop off our children at school while listening to a tape to learn French, dressed in a jogging suit because we are pressing to get to our aerobics class by 9:00, but we're taking the longer route that enables us to drop off the Express Mail along the way. It's immediate results we are after, so what exactly is the cash value, the payoff, of prayer? Cost-benefits are all that count, and even there a "long-term" view is three to six months. So to be committed to commitment, let alone developing a slow-maturing relationship, whether it is with God, our children or anyone else, is in direct conflict with our culture.

Just to develop a solid relationship with your child, one anthropologist says, "you've got to hang around with your kids." The same could be said for our relationship with God. Yet hanging-around time is the first thing to go in the frantic schedules we keep. "Sure enough the computers are byting, the satellites spinning, the Cuisinarts whizzing, just as planned. Yet we are ever out of breath. 'It is ironic,' writes social theorist Jeremy Rifkin in *Time Wars*, 'that in a culture so committed to saving time we feel increasingly deprived of the very thing we value.'"[1]

Let's face it. Modern culture is not going to give us the time we need to develop a relationship with God. So we confront a choice. We cannot hope for support, but it is important that we know what we are up against and what's at stake. To take time in one's day for prayer and Bible reading is an anachronism in modern culture. It has about the same professional status and prospective benefits as an ambition to become a career shepherd. But at least we know where we are. Support and understanding are out, but the still center is a priority all the same.

His Eye Still on the Sparrow

How does God sustain us in our love for him and demonstrate that resurrection power? Sometimes it is in simple ways, such as an encouragement through reading a verse from the Bible. A friend of mine discovered that her husband was having an affair. He was a fairly well-known minister. To add more fuel to her pain, she had never had a close relationship with her own father. Her father was an emotionally distant man who was never involved with her life. She had never felt chosen by him. Now she was in a marriage in which not only was she not chosen, she had been rejected for someone else.

Mary told me that one morning she awoke full of the pain of rejection that had current as well as childhood roots. She had a deep faith, so she poured out to God her anguish and despair. She said to God, "I wish I could find a word to express exactly how I am feeling; a word that would express the depth of my sorrow." Suddenly a word came to her. It was a word she had never used before. She knew it was a word from God. It was the word *forsaken*.

"Yes, Lord," she said. "That's exactly it. I feel forsaken. How I wish I knew what it's like to be someone's bride. To be cherished and loved. How I wish I knew what it's like to be someone's daughter."

She then turned to her Bible readings for the day, and here were the words she read: "No longer shall they call thee Forsaken . . . for the Lord delighteth in thee. Thy Maker is thine husband, the Lord of hosts is his name. And as a bridegroom rejoiceth over the bride, so shall the Lord rejoice over thee. He hath sent me . . . to comfort all that mourn, . . . to give them beauty for ashes, the oil of joy for their mourning, the garment of praise for the spirit of heaviness. . . . Cast your cares upon me, for your heavenly father careth for you."

When God reaches a person in that way, who could feel forsaken?

No More Beating Down with Negatives

A story from my own life comes to mind. One day while I was living in Israel I took the bus to go home from downtown Jerusalem, but I inadvertently got off at the wrong stop and was promptly lost—not an unusual state of affairs for me. I began peering around at street signs to discover where I was. Suddenly I heard a voice behind me say in slightly halting English, "Can I help you?"

I turned around and to my astonishment saw an Orthodox Hasidic Jew. He was a vision in black, dressed in the attire typical of the Orthodox community of his eighteenth-century Polish predecessors: a long black coat over black trousers, a long white fringe hanging from his belt, bearded with earlocks that came down to his chest, pale skin reflecting the Hasidic male's devotion to the intense daily indoor study of Torah. It is hard to convey to Western Gentiles how extraordinary it is for a Hasidic man from the ultraorthodox neighborhood of Meah Shearim to speak to a woman, particularly a Western woman. They live by an immense number of rules that regulate every dimension of behavior, and male-female interaction is especially controlled.

I probably could not conceal the amazement on my face, and he said, "Sometimes we are permitted to help people in distress. Where do you need to go?" To my further astonishment he accompanied me on the street and told me his name was Moshe and that he lived in an ultraorthodox community in Jerusalem, although he was raised in Chicago. His accent indicated that he spoke more Yiddish and Hebrew than English.

I tried to establish some common ground but found that our worlds were so dramatically different that small talk was impossible. I decided to take a different tactic.

"We do share something in common," I said.

"What is that?" he asked.

"We are both religious," I exclaimed.

"That's wonderful!" he shouted in reply, and immediately began a discourse on one of the tractates from the Mishnah. Then he noticed that I had paused, and he said, "Are you Jewish?"

"No, I am a follower of Jesus," I answered.

"Are you serious about your faith?" he asked. I assured him that I was.

"This is fascinating," he said. "I have never talked with a religious Christian before. There is much that I would like to ask you, but it is so difficult. If anyone in my community saw me holding a long conversation with you it could be very awkward. I have to be so careful. Yet when will I have this opportunity again? Oh, I don't expect you to understand. You *goyim* wouldn't understand our ways. But would it interest you to have a religious dialogue?" he asked nervously.

"I would love to talk with you!" I answered, sensing how sincere he was. But I could also see his discomfort as he constantly peered over his shoulder to see if anyone was watching us.

I took a deep breath and said, "I would be honored to have you as a guest in my home."

He hesitated, glanced around and said in a cloak-and-dagger manner, "Let us go quickly." So off we went to my apartment, my ultraorthodox friend with his earlocks flying in the breeze and me.

Once we were seated in my living room he began to pepper me with questions about what it means to be a follower of Jesus. His questions were theologically astute and probing. There were two things that interested him the most. First, he wanted to know what happened to human nature as a result of being in relationship with God through Christ. I explained that when we come to put our faith in God, he gives us his Spirit, who transforms us day by day and enables us to live as new people with a new power.

"What is the essence of this new nature?" he asked. So I quickly went over the list of the "fruit of the Spirit" from Paul's letter to the Galatians and started to go on.

"Wait! Say those words again," he responded. So I recited them again.

"Say them again," he asked. I did.

"What beautiful, beautiful words," he said. "Love, joy, peace, patience, kindness, goodness, faithfulness, gentleness and self-control. Imagine it! All of these qualities come into your heart as a result of being in relationship with God. Just think, to receive the very nature of God as a gift. No more beating down the evil inclinations with negatives but rather fighting evil with positives, with the very attributes of God himself! Ah, what a precious gift you have inherited, Becky. Do not take it lightly."

He was doubly right. They are a precious gift, and we do often take them lightly. I went on. "Please don't think I'm suggesting that all of these qualities are mastered by us overnight. Living the resurrection isn't magic. We don't turn to God in faith and suddenly plug into all of these qualities. They are cultivated over time, through obedience and through the grace of God."

"Of course I know it can't happen quickly," he mused. "We are still human beings who by nature are self-centered and self-absorbed. But what hope it must give, to have God's power working in you to enable you to forgo the old ways and live the new way."

I could not remember when I had heard a simpler or more eloquent explanation of the meaning of Christian conversion than from this Orthodox Jewish friend sitting in my living room.

What also interested him was how I sensed the presence of God in my life. Then I told him a story of how God had helped me through a recent time of crisis and fear by giving me just the right word from Scripture. I had awakened one morning feeling overwhelmed by fear, but then I read the appointed Bible verses for that day in my devotional: "Be strong and courageous. Do not be terrified; do not be discouraged, for the Lord your God will be with you wherever you go" (Joshua 1:9). Suddenly he clapped his hands together, stood up and to my amazement shouted, "That's it! That is it! That is what it is all about. My daughter, you have it. Only God could have given you those words at just that time." It was an indescribably joyful moment.

The only sad note in our conversation was the ending, because he told me that we could never meet again. He instructed me that if I should see him on the street, I was not to acknowledge him, for it would endanger his stance in the community. But he said, "We have begun a friendship of faith, Becky. I will not forget what we have talked about—not ever." And he left, leaving me far richer for the experience.

God's means of grace are dynamic and alive. They touch not only the recipients but even those with whom we come into contact.

Forgiving When We Hate

Let's move on to an even harder instance of the power of the resurrection. What do we do when we hate the "neighbor" we are supposed to love? Back in Portland, Oregon, I first heard Corrie ten Boom tell a story that has always been to me an extraordinary demonstration of the power of new life. During World War II and the Nazi occupation of Holland, she had endured horrors of many sorts and humiliation from the guards in the concentration camp.

When she came onto the stage in Portland, her opening remark was "I don't want you to take any notes or listen to anything I say unless you know who I am." The audience began to chuckle softly, because everyone knew who Corrie was.

Then she proceeded, "My name is Corrie ten Boom and I am a murderer." There was total silence. "You see, when I was in prison camp I saw the same guard day in and day out. He was the one who mocked and sneered at us when we were stripped naked and taken into the showers. He spat on us in contempt, and I hated him. I hated him with every fiber of my being. And Jesus says when you hate someone you are guilty of murder. So I wanted you to know right from the start that you are listening to a murderer.

"When we were freed, I left Germany vowing never to return," she continued. "But I was invited back there to speak. I didn't want to go, but I felt the Lord nudging me to. Very reluctantly I went. My first talk was on forgiveness. Suddenly, as I was speaking, I saw to my horror that same prison guard sitting in the audience. There was no way that he would have recognized me. When he had last seen me, I was emaciated, sick, and my hair was shorn. But I could never forget his face, never. It was clear to me from the radiant look on his face while I spoke that he had been converted since I saw him last. After I had finished speaking he came up and said with a beaming smile, 'Ah, dear sister Corrie, isn't it wonderful how God forgives?' And he extended his hand for me to shake."

"All I felt as I looked at him was hate. I said to the Lord silently, 'There is nothing in me that could ever love that man. I hate him for what he did to me and to my family. But you tell us that we are to love our enemies. That's impossible for me, but nothing is impossible for you. So if you expect me to love this man, it's going to have to come from you, because all I feel is hate.'"

She told us that at that moment she felt nudged to do only one thing. "Put out your hand, Corrie," the Lord seemed to say. She said, "It took all of the years that I had quietly obeyed God in obscurity to do the hardest thing I have ever done in my life. I put out my hand." Then she said something remarkable happened. "It was only after my simple act of obedience that I felt something almost like warm oil was being poured over me. And with it came the unmistakable message: 'Well done, Corrie. That's how my children behave.' And the hate in my heart was absorbed and gone. And so one murderer embraced another murderer, but in the love of Christ."

Then Corrie, in her wonderful Dutch accent, said, "Yes, I am a murderer. But you are listening to one gloriously, marvelously freed and forgiven murderer. You see, I love so much because I have been forgiven of so much!"

Corrie's story is unusual. Most of us have not had to face the evil and endure the pain that she did. Perhaps that is why God reached out to her so immediately and quickly. But again, the point is to see how practical and how extraordinary living the resurrection is. God takes the enormity of sin and evil so seriously and is so concerned to respond to it that he shook the foundations of the universe. In Christ he suffered death on the cross. *Living* the cross and the resurrection is made possible for us *because of* the cross and resurrection. God will help us to do what we must do but could never do on our own.

Walking in the Dark

So far all of these stories have been about faith making a decisive difference. But does faith always "work"? What about the times when God does not seem to come through? When we are bitterly disappointed or feel abandoned or frustrated that something does not change even though we have asked repeatedly for God's help? What do we say to someone who says, "I've turned my life over to God but it doesn't seem to be working for me"?

One thing is clear from Christian testimonies. Different things change for people at different times and in different ways. Some people meet God and are changed dramatically. They are so transformed that we can hardly believe the difference when we see them. Others experience change more like a refinement that takes place slowly over time. Only God knows the reasons why that is so, and to pretend otherwise is presumptuous and cruel.

But what of situations where there seems to be no change at all and we are completely in the dark? What kind of realistic hope are we to hold to? There are three things I have found helpful in facing that question. First, there is the question of our basic expectations. We live, as we saw earlier, in the "between times." Over much that we desire and much for which we pray are the two words *Not Yet.* So we pray and work for change and growth. But remembering that we still live in a broken, fallen world, we do not expect complete change or total transformation. Yet we should expect what Francis Schaeffer used to call "substantial healing"—in other words, a change that is substantial and significant, though always short of the total change we will experience only on the other side of death, when we see God face to face.

Second, there is the question of our part. Have we obeyed everything God has shown us? Have we done everything we know to effect change? We need to be brutally honest with ourselves. There are too many cases of people who love biblical truth yet do not live it. There are too many who say they believe in forgiveness yet seek every escape hatch rather than forgive someone who has wronged them. There are too many who are able to quote Jesus and St. Paul but who do not follow what they say. In short, there are too many Christians with loud protestations of a longing to be changed, yet too few willing to do what it takes.

Third, there is the question of God's part—or more accurately, our response to having no idea what God's part is. How are we to trust when we are completely in the dark? What faith needs then is what Os Guinness in his book *Doubt* calls the principle of "suspended judgment." Is this another word for our old enemies, denial and irrationality? Not at all. Here is how Guinness puts it: "As believers, we cannot always know why, but we can always know why we trust God who knows why." He reminds Christians what this means. "A Christian does not say, 'I do not understand you at all, but I will trust you anyway.' Rather, he says, 'I do not understand you in this situation, but I understand why I trust you anyway. Therefore I can trust that you understand even though I don't.'"[2] The principle of suspended judgment means that we may be in the dark about some situations, but we are not in the dark about God.

Who Is the Innocent?

It is now time to think back to my professor friend in the first chapter who asked me what difference faith makes. This was my answer:

"Do you remember just now when you swore and then said, 'Oh, excuse me, Becky!' That was a kind gesture. But isn't your underlying assumption that since I am religious I am therefore innocent and need protection from the big bad world out there?

"Excuse me for being so direct, but I think you've got it backwards. You're the innocent, not me, if you assume that. What constitutes badness for you would seem like pretty tame stuff to me. You do not understand. I am religious *precisely* because I am not innocent. The Bible tells me I never was. My faith in God comes from knowing that I am in trouble, I am flawed, and I need outside help to be changed."

"You seem pretty nice to me," he answered.

"Yes, but that is where the difference begins to show. I could do a good deed and you would think that was great. But I would think differently, for I have seen that I can do the nicest things for the most selfish of reasons. And I have been given a diagnosis for my condition: It is called sin."

"Then why do you seem so upbeat? If I were that hard on myself, I'd be depressed," he said.

"Because it's a relief to not have to pretend that I don't have a problem and because I've been given a solution: the forgiveness and love of God through Jesus Christ," I said.

"Has the solution worked? You seem so joyful."

"I'm not a finished product, if that's what you mean. But I am learning to live in recovery from sin and I'm growing in grace, and that would make anybody hopeful."

Uncle Roger's Moment

Whenever one speaks or writes on Christian themes in much of the Western world, the biggest problem is not skepticism but sentimentalism. Convictions have been transformed into clichés. Christian truths are unknown, because they are too well known. This can easily happen even to truths like the resurrection. Yet when the chips are down, only the toughest convictions carry weight—and nowhere is this truer than with death.

Our Christian hope is not for this life only. Paul wrote to the Corinthians, "If Christ has not been raised, . . . we are to be pitied more than all men" (1 Corinthians 15:17-19). He was addressing the central question of life: what does life mean if the end is death? Writing to the Thessalonians about loved ones who have died, Paul tells us, "We do not . . . grieve like the rest of men, who have no hope. We believe that Jesus died and rose again and so we believe that God will bring with Jesus those who have fallen asleep in him . . . and so we will be with the Lord forever" (1 Thessalonians 4:13-14, 17).

If there is nothing beyond the grave, then life on this side is diminished too. It does not last long enough or amount to enough to be worthwhile in itself. It would provide no redress of injustice, no fulfillment of joy and no reason to forfeit instant gratification. If this is all there is, then our attempts to give ourselves and life significance merely seem like pathetic clutching. But the Bible insists that we have significance, that life means something, because even after death we still are, and more to the point, we are what *we have chosen.*

The Bible affirms that each person has eternal significance. We will all live eternally. The issue is whether we live eternally in relationship with God or, if we so tragically choose, without him. That is the why the resurrection of Christ is so important. He conquered death and in doing so offers us the possibility of life forever in the presence of God.

When C. S. Lewis lost his wife, Joy, to cancer, his faith was tested beyond anything he had previously experienced. He was emotionally shattered, and he describes his feelings in the book *A Grief Observed*. It is one long, honest scream of pain. "They tell me she is at peace. What makes them so sure?" But as he goes through his "dark night of the soul," his faith emerges and triumphs over his grief. Several things become clear to him: "If she is not now, then she never was. I mistook a cloud of atoms for a person. And if life ends at death, then it does not amount to very much."[3]

That is a point that many miss. What we decide about eternity shapes our view of life. The knowledge that life is eternal means that life becomes vastly more important. It means that the choices, the triumphs, the victories of this world matter terribly and are eternal in nature. And so do the defeats and moral failures. If life is eternal, then all that we do, both for good and for evil, has eternal consequence.

Conversely, the hope of unbelievers, or those who have much to regret and no way to escape it, is that there will be no life beyond the grave. For them, life ending with eternal darkness is the final escape, where no wrong is lasting, no sin goes on for eternity. Skeptics may view life as ultimately trivial, but at least there are no lasting consequences for the choices they make. But if they are wrong, if in fact life's boundaries reach to eternity, then who we are and what we do is tremendously important. Then the good and evil we do are blown up to eternity's size.

Never was the awesome importance of what we decide more poignant to me than in the death of my Uncle Roger, the kindest, warmest man I have ever known. A marathon runner and the picture of health, he was abruptly diagnosed as having terminal lung cancer at the age of sixty. We hoped against hope that the chemotherapy would prove effective, but the cancer spread too rapidly. One morning I received a call from my mother telling me he was not expected to live through the day. Only one thought plagued me: Though he was a wonderful man, by his own admission he had not put his faith in God. Now it seemed too late. I could not get home to Illinois soon enough to talk with him, and he was lapsing into a semicoma. But the thought that I would not share eternity with him in God's presence was more than I could bear. There was only one thing to do—pray.

I called one of my best friends, with whom I pray frequently. She is one of the most spiritually sensitive people I have ever known, and what she told me left me stunned. She said she had awakened in the middle of the night feeling burdened to pray for someone in danger. But she did not know who or what was involved. She went downstairs and began to pray and read the Bible. As she prayed, she felt the Spirit of God, along with the passages she was reading, confirm that someone was dying and she was supposed to pray for that person. She wanted to go back to bed but could not shake the desperate sense of need. Again she got out of bed and went downstairs to pray until dawn. Then came my call a few hours later.

So my friend and I prayed. We prayed that God would not let Roger die before he had clearly heard the message of the gospel and that he would receive it and believe. Throughout the day I was in touch with my family. The medical news was always the same. He was still in a semicoma, eyes closed, saying nothing. My handsome, always smiling, athletic six-foot uncle had in only four months become emaciated, bald, like an old man. He was breathing through a mask, and his doctors thought he would not last the day.

I did nothing but pray and fast. My friend did the same. We begged God to let him live so he could hear and believe. But who would tell him? What possible good would it do with him in a coma? Never mind, we kept praying.

That night my mother called and said, "No one can believe it, but Roger was suddenly alert, eyes opened and talking. Now the doctors wonder if he might have more like a month or so to live."

I began planning my trip home but continued to pray that God would send a messenger to Roger. But his alertness lasted only that evening—thankfully giving him time to talk to his wife and children. Then he sank again. It was now very clear that death was not far away.

The next day he stayed in his semicoma state, totally unable to communicate. My friend and I prayed and fasted all of that day too. I walked through a park, asking God for the same thing we had ever since we received the news—for Roger to revive long enough to hear the message and for someone on the spot to take the initiative to talk to him.

Then something remarkable happened. A hometown doctor, Roger Weiss, who was a friend of the family and a Christian, felt an inner urge to go to the hospital and explain the gospel to Uncle Roger. When he called he was told that a visit was probably not possible because Roger's condition had deteriorated, but throughout the day Dr. Weiss could not shake the urge. He became convinced that God was leading him to go, even though Uncle Roger was in a coma. Finally he called the family and said, "I'm coming anyway. I'll be there in ten minutes."

At 4:55 Roger suddenly woke up out of the coma and smiled, and the first thing he did was ask about his mother, for whom he was concerned. He was totally alert. Nurses began flying around. No one could believe he had revived again. At 5:00 p.m. in walked Dr. Weiss.

For the next twenty minutes Dr. Weiss talked with Uncle Roger. He told him, "You are one of the finest men I have known. But have you done things wrong in your life, Roger? Things you truly regret?"

"Oh, yes, so many," Roger said.

"Jesus came to forgive the wrong we've done," the doctor said. "He died to put it right because, as good as you are, being good isn't enough. We have all fallen short of God's standards. We are all guilty of not making him the center of our lives. Jesus is here. He wants to reach out to you, even in this last hour. He longs to forgive you. But you are the only one who can make that decision. The ball is in your court. Do you understand everything I am saying?"

"Yes," answered Roger. "I just wish you had told me this sooner." There was a moment of silence, and Roger said, "I'm not ready yet. I need more time to think about it."

Dr. Weiss answered warmly, "God loves you so much, he may give you more time. I pray that he will." That was the last time he saw Roger alive.

While Roger was still alert the family was able to say goodbye. A few hours later, my mother, Sue, Uncle Roger's only sibling, came in. "Do you remember when Dr. Weiss was here and what he talked about?" she asked.

"Yes, I do." he responded.

"I just want you to know that I can't bear the thought of spending eternity without you either."

He smiled and thanked her, saying, "I'm still thinking about it."

Shortly after that he went back into a semicoma. His daughter and wife stayed by his side throughout the night. He spoke incoherently, reliving the past as his mind wandered freely.

My aunt slipped out of the room for a few minutes. Suddenly Roger looked directly at his daughter, Megan, and said in a clear voice and with clear eyes, "Meg, did you see him when he came to visit me?"

"Did I see whom, Daddy?" she asked.

"He came to me. He came right here to my bed. He spoke to me. Father."

Since these were the first coherent words he had spoken for hours, and since no one in the family referred to the deceased grandfather as anything but Daddy, Meg felt something extraordinary had happened.

"Dad," she said. "I'm not sure what you mean. But I have something very important to tell you. It means everything to me. Do you remember what Dr. Weiss and Sue talked to you about?"

"Yes, I do," he answered.

"Dad, I hope you will choose to give your life to Jesus."

He did not speak for a moment. Then he said, "I already have, Meg. I asked him. I said yes."

Those were the last coherent words Roger ever spoke. He slipped into a deep coma. The next morning my mom came to stay with him. She held the hand of her only brother and eased him into death. "Jesus is here, Roger. He loves you so. He'll take you home now. You've suffered enough. Just put your hand in his. It's time to go home." And he died.

As Roger died, I was in an airplane on my way to Champaign, Illinois. The one thing I prayed for, aside from his salvation, was that if he had decided to choose God we would know. The day of my flight I changed my reservations three times. I felt as if I were in a total fog. When I had to change planes in Ohio, I called home to see if there was any news. Mother told me that Uncle Roger had just died, but he had died a believer.

I can safely say that I have rarely worshiped God in more purity and fullness than I did at that moment, standing in front of the pay telephone with tears streaming down my face. To think that a dying man could say, "I need more time," and God would give it to him. He brought a doctor from out of nowhere and woke Roger up from a coma, all because he loved him and because the choice was that critical. Dr. Weiss said it was a celestial commando raid to reach Roger.

As I boarded the plane on that last leg of the flight to Champaign, I thought, *If only I could share this moment and tell someone who means something to me what God has done.* I fumbled for my ticket with tear-stained eyes to see my seat assignment. I sat down, sighed deeply and looked over at the passenger in the seat next to me. There to my utter astonishment was my brother, Bob, on his way from Miami to Champaign. That we would end up next to each other on a plane in Ohio is something only God could have arranged.

This deeply personal story reveals much of what God is like. It also reveals the means of grace that God used to reach my uncle: the Spirit of God that awakened my friend to pray, that moved Dr. Weiss to talk to Uncle Roger even though it seemed absurd under the circumstances. It also reveals the critical importance of the will, how terribly important our decision of faith is. But most of all it's a story about a God who loves us and reaches out to us.

At Uncle Roger's funeral we read from the book of Revelation:

"Who are they, and where did they come from?" . . .

And he said, "These are they who have come out of the great tribulation;
they have washed their robes and made them white in the blood of the
Lamb. . . .

"Never again will they hunger;
  never again will they thirst.
The sun will not beat upon them,
  nor any scorching heat.
For the Lamb at the center of the throne will be their shepherd;
  he will lead them to springs of living water.
And God will wipe away every tear from their eyes." (Revelation 7:13-17)

Yes, we as a family grieved. Our hearts were broken because we loved
Roger so. But never have the words rung truer to me: "We do not grieve as
those who have no hope."

Christians are people of hope and not despair. Because we know that
God, who had the first word, will have the last. He is never thwarted or
caught napping by the circumstances of our lives. To have faith in Jesus
does not mean we try to pretend that bad things are really good. Rather, we
know that God will take our difficulties and weave them into purposes we
cannot see as yet. And when he is done, the day will be more glorious for
our having gone through the difficulties. We are not unmindful of the difference between what is evil and what is good. We know that if the logic of
his love nailed Jesus to the cross, we have no right to go another way.

But our lives can be lived well, with courage and with joy, because we
live by the hope of the resurrection. So no matter what life lands in our
laps, if we will only trust God and wait and never lose heart, the song we
sing one day will be of victory. And then, with battles over, the time will
come when faith becomes sight and hope fulfillment and our whole beings
are united with the God we love. Joy of all joys, goal of our desire, all that
we long for will be ours, for we will be his.

For the moment, though, we are still on the road. The gap between
promise and performance is still the tension of our faith. Yet hope in Christ
is the most compelling incentive in the world. Hope has its reasons after all.

Notes

Chapter 1: The Problem with the World Is Me

[1]"Whatever Happened to Ethics?" *Time*, May 1987, pp. 14-29.

[2]Gary Trudeau, commencement address at Colby College, Waterville, Maine, May 28, 1981.

[3]Ted Koppel, commencement address at Duke University, as quoted in "Education: Now, a Few Words from the Wise," *Time*, June 22, 1987, p. 69.

[4]Mona Charen, "Sin, Anyone?" *The Washington Post*, March 27, 2000.

[5]James Davison Hunter, "When Psychotherapy Replaces Religion," *The Public Interest* (spring 2000).

Chapter 2: The Lie That We're OK

[1]Albert Camus, *The Fall* (New York: Alfred A. Knopf, 1957). Quotes in this chapter are from pages 14, 108, 59-60, 84, 47, 81, 110, respectively.

[2]David H. Malan, *Individual Psychotherapy and the Science of Psychodynamics* (London: Butterworth, 1979), p. 15.

[3]Robert I. Lifton, *The Nazi Doctors* (New York: Basic Books, 1986). Quotes in this chapter are from pages 8 and 321, respectively.

[4]Meg Greenfield, "The No-Fault Confession," *Newsweek*, June 15, 1987, p. 50.

[5]Kenneth Woodward, "Heaven: This Is the Season to Search for New Meaning in Old Familiar Places," *Newsweek*, March 27, 1989, pp. 52-53.

Chapter 3: The Lie That We're in Charge

[1]Albert Camus, *The Fall* (New York: Alfred A. Knopf, 1957). Quotes in this chapter are from pages 48, 49, 56, respectively.

[2]Bertrand Russell, *Power: A New Social Analysis* (New York: W. W. Norton, 1969). Quotes in this chapter are from page 11.

[3]G. K. Chesterton, *Orthodoxy* (New York: Doubleday, 1973). Quotes in this chapter are from page 144.

[4]Reinhold Niebuhr, *The Nature and Destiny of Man* (New York: Charles Scribner's Sons, 1949). Quotes in this chapter are from pages 192, 189, 174, respectively.

[5]Ernest Becker, *The Denial of Death* (New York: Free Press, 1973). Quotes in this chapter are from pages 56, 55, 52, 265, respectively.

[6]Wilhelm Reich, *The Mass Psychology of Fascism* (New York: Farrar, Straus & Giroux, 1970), p. 334.

[7]Blaise Pascal, *Pensées*, ed. Louis Lafuma, trans. A. I. Krailsheimer (New York: Penguin, 1966), p. 55.

[8]C. S. Lewis, *The Problem of Pain* (New York: Macmillan, 1978), p. 44.

[9]Karl Marx, quoted in Becker, *Denial of Death*, p. 265.

[10]Fred Bruning, "Easy Solutions in the New Age," *McClean's*, March 21, 1988, pp. 9-10.

[11]Shirley MacLaine, cited in Fred Bruning, "Easy Solutions in the New Age."

Chapter 4: Worshiping the Wrong Things
[1]Ernest Becker, *The Denial of Death* (New York: Free Press, 1973). Quotes in this chapter are from pages 150, 160, 261, 193, respectively.
[2]Blaise Pascal, *Pensées*, ed. Louis Lafuma, trans. A. I. Krailsheimer (New York: Penguin, 1966), p. 65.
[3]Albert Camus, *The Fall* (New York: Alfred A. Knopf, 1957). Quotes in this chapter are from pages 102, 99, 100, 108-9, 82, 144-45, respectively.
[4]Peter Shaffer, *Equus* (New York: Avon, 1974): Quotes in this chapter are from pages 94, 124, 93, 95, respectively.
[5]Wallace Stevens, "Sunday Morning," in *Selected Poems* (New York: Faber, 1986), p. 32.
[6]F. Scott Fitzgerald, *Tender Is the Night* (Harmondsworth, U.K.: Penguin, 1934), p. 323.
[7]John Cheever, "The Sorrows of Gin," in *The Short Stories of John Cheever* (New York: Ballantine, 1985), p. 248.
[8]"Moral Issues as Seen Through Fiction," class held at Harvard School of Business, taught by Dr. Robert Coles, fall 1986.
[9]Fyodor Dostoyevski, *The Brothers Karamazov*, trans. Michael Komroff (New York: Signet Classic, 1957), pp. 233, 235.
[10]C. S. Lewis, *The Screwtape Letters* (New York: Macmillan, 1961), p. 38.
[11]Simone de Beauvoir, quoted in Herbert R. Lottman, *Albert Camus: A Biography* (London: Weidenfeld & M. Colson, 1979), p. 578.
[12]Albert Camus, quoted in ibid., p. 564.
[13]Quoted by M. Scott Peck, "Door Interview," *Wittenburg Door*, no. 74 (1983): 18-25. Peck does not identify the Brazilian psychiatrist other than by surname.

Chapter 5: Who Can Tell Me What Is Wrong?
[1]Joseph R. Cooke, *Free for the Taking* (Old Tappan, N.J.: Revell, 1975), p. 68.
[2]Ernest Becker, *The Denial of Death* (New York: Free Press, 1973). Quotes in this chapter are from pages 2, 164, 198, respectively.
[3]Robert Coles, "Storytellers' Ethics," *Harvard Business Review*, March-April 1987, p. 14.
[4]Flannery O'Connor, *Mystery and Manners* (New York: Farrar, Straus & Giroux, 1969).
[5]Blaise Pascal, *Pensées*, ed. Louis Lafuma, trans. A. J. Krailsheimer (New York: Penguin, 1966). Quotes in this chapter are from page 65.
[6]Albert Camus, *The Plague* (New York: Modern Library, 1948), p. 278.
[7]Barbara Tuchman, *The March of Folly* (New York: Ballantine, 1984), p. 5.
[8]Ruth Burrows, *To Believe in Jesus* (Denville, N.J.: Dimension, 1978), p. 3.
[9]Albert Camus, *The Fall* (New York: Alfred A. Knopf, 1957), p. 81.

Chapter 6: The Cross
[1]F. Scott Fitzgerald, *Tender Is the Night* (Harmondsworth, U.K.: Penguin, 1934), p. 335.
[2]E. H. Gifford, cited in Leon Morris, *The Atonement* (Downers Grove, Ill.: InterVarsity Press, 1983), p. 147.
[3]Victor Hugo, *Les Miserables*, trans. Lee Fahnstock and Norman MacAfee (New York: New American Library, 1987). Quotes in this chapter are from pages 90, 1322, 1323, 105, 106, 110, 113, respectively.
[4]John R. W. Stott, *The Cross of Christ* (Downers Grove, Ill.: InterVarsity Press, 1986). Quotes in

this chapter are from pages 159, 160, 162, respectively.

[5]Reinhold Niebuhr, *The Nature and Destiny of Man* (New York: Charles Scribner's Sons, 1964), p. 142.

[6]Millard Erickson, *Christian Theology* (Grand Rapids, Mich.: Baker, 1983), p. 788.

[7]Sebastian Moore, *The Crucified Jesus Is No Stranger* (San Francisco: Harper & Row, 1977), p. 3.

[8]Gerald May, *Will and Spirit* (San Francisco: Harper & Row, 1982), p. 1.

Chapter 7: The Resurrection
[1]Harville Hendrix, *Getting the Love You Want* (New York: Henry Holt, 1988), p. 13.

[2]Raymond E. Brown, *The Gospel According to John 13-21* (New York: Doubleday, 1970), p. 1035.

[3]Eugene H. Peterson, *Traveling Light* (Downers Grove, Ill.: InterVarsity Press, 1982), p. 20.

[4]C. S. Lewis, *The Weight of Glory* (New York: Macmillan, 1980), pp. 15-16.

[5]Eugene H. Peterson, *Reversed Thunder* (San Francisco: Harper & Row, 1988), p. 146.

[6]Richard Harries, *Prayer and the Pursuit of Happiness* (London: Fount, 1985), pp. 142-43.

[7]Lewis, *Weight of Glory*, p. 4.

[8]Flannery O'Connor, *The Complete Stories* (New York: Farrar, Straus & Giroux, 1971), p. 131.

Chapter 8: How Do We Change?
[1]Flannery O'Connor, *Three by Flannery O'Connor* (New York: New American Library, 1962), p. 21.

[2]Robert J. Lifton, *The Nazi Doctors* (New York: Basic Books, 1986), p. 502.

[3]Martin Luther, *Meditations on the Gospels*, trans. Roland Bainton (Philadelphia: Westminster Press, 1962).

[4]John Stott, *Confess Your Sins* (Waco, Tex.: Word, 1974), p. 13.

[5]Joseph R. Cooke, *Free for the Taking* (Old Tappan, N.J.: Revell, 1975), p. 8.

[6]Lovelace Howard, "The Evangelical Catholic" (The Evangelical and Catholic Mission in the Episcopal Church, August 1988), p. 4.

[7]C. S. Lewis, *Surprised by Joy* (New York: Harcourt Brace, 1956), pp. 228-29.

Chapter 9: Living the Cross
[1]Blaise Pascal, *Pensées,* ed. Louis Lafuma, trans. A. I. Krailsheimer (New York: Penguin, 1966), p. 498.

[2]Peter Kreeft, *Making Sense out of Suffering* (Ann Arbor, Mich.: Servant, 1986).

[3]Fulton Sheen, *Congressional Record,* 96th Congress, 1st session, 2951.

Chapter 10: Living the Resurrection
[1]Jeremy Rifkin, quoted in Nancy Gibbs, "How America Has Run Out of Time," *Time,* April 24, 1989, p. 59.

[2]Os Guinness, *Doubt* (Batavia, Ill.: Lion, 1976), pp. 204-6.

[3]C. S. Lewis, *A Grief Observed* (San Francisco: Harper & Row, 1989), pp. 24-25.